FLORIDA STATE
UNIVERSITY LIBRARIES

MAY 7 2001

TALLAHASSEE, FLORIDA

HUMANE ECONOMY

HUMANE ECONOMY

JAN SOLLENIUS

ALMQVIST & WIKSELL INTERNATIONAL

First published in 2000
by Almqvist & Wiksell International
Stockholm, Sweden

© Copyright 2000. All rights reserved.
No part of this book may be reproduced in any form without permission,
except for the quotation of brief passages in criticism.

ISBN 91-22-01874-3

Printed by Elanders Gotab AB, Stockholm

CONTENTS

INTRODUCTION	7
A POSSIBLE NEW CRISIS	15
THE PROMISING BOOM	15
THE POLITICAL FACTOR: RUSSIA	21
A NEW RECESSION?	35
TOWARDS A SOLUTION	45
PRACTICAL ELEMENTS OF SYNTHESES	45
MONETARIST TENETS	53
NEW-OLD CLASSICALS	59
KEYNESIAN DIFFERENCES	71
NO "NATURAL RATE"	89
MIXED ECONOMY	105
WELFARE SERVICES	117
THE PUBLIC SECTOR AS REMEDY	131
COMBINED KEYNESIAN EXPANSION	137
NONINFLATIONARY MONETIZATION REVISITED	147
"DIRECT MONETIZATION"	148
EXTERNAL PUBLIC DEBT	165
DEBT WITHIN THE PUBLIC SECTOR	167
MONETIZATION IN GENERAL	171
PRUDENT MONETARY EXPANSION	177
SMALL-STEP MONETIZATION	177
ENDOGENOUS MONEY SUPPLY	181
ADVICE TO THE EU	193
RESTRAINING INFLATION	199
INCOMES AGREEMENTS	199
CONSUMER BOYCOTTS	207
REFERENCES	209

The publication of this work was supported by the

Swedish Council for Social Research

INTRODUCTION

In recent years I have been strengthened, I feel, in my old conviction that there are no sharp demarcation lines whatsoever between various disciplines within the social sciences. Any boundary is blurred, I think, and the disciplines pervade each other fairly deeply. This is very true of economics, even if some economists of a "chauvinist" inclination might feel somewhat hurt by this idea. Various factors that have often been considered either political or economic aspects of society, separately, as well as psychological or sociological aspects in their own right, are in fact much more interwoven than many devoted economists like to believe. Economics has much to do with and is rather deeply influenced by political science and indeed by the politics of the real world, and these influences are mutual, for that matter. One can refer, for example, to Swedberg (1997:168) about 'political embeddedness', to Greider (1995) about economics and ideology, to Howitt (1990:76) about the fact that "(a)nti-Keynesian economics is part of the more general neoconservative movement that gained force in the 1970s", or to Korpi (1996a:1727, 1742) about "objectivity sclerosis" for political reasons.

The intertwining of economic processes with psychological phenomena has been recognized by numerous authors, among them no less an economist than Keynes himself (1936:150-151, 154-155, 159, 161-163, 172, 246-247, 250-254, 317). There are economists with a strong interest in psychology, for example, Katona (1975) or Scitovsky (1986, 1992, 1995: Chapters 5 and 12). It is also interesting to read the opinion of Ritter and Silber (1993:426-427) when, analysing the presuppositions of the rational expectations trend, they say that "(a)t this point our discussion of the trade-off between inflation and unemployment sounds more like topics in advanced psychology than anything resembling economic policy". Economics also has quite a lot in common with history, as we know from Hobsbawm (1997: Chapters 7 and 8), and much in common with moral philosophy, as we know from Etzioni (1988) and also from the Nobel laureate Amartya Sen (see, for instance, 1970 with mathematical methods, and 1987a, 1987b and 1993).

Last but not least, economics has a great deal in common with sociology; there is a growing interdisciplinary zone between them. Economic sociology is defined by Smelser and Swedberg (1994a:3) "most simply as the sociological perspective applied to economic phenomena". A good example is Ingham's (1998) study of the "Sociology of Money". As he (Ingham 1998:4) says, "(m)oney ... is not only socially produced, but is a social relation (Ingham 1996)". It is obvious that, as Swedberg and Granovetter (1992:1) write, "sooner or later the realization was bound to come that it was unwise to make such a sharp separation between what is 'economic' and what is 'social'". Kalleberg (1995:1216) points out that "(i)ntegrating sociology and economics is possible because these disciplines are complementary in many ways". We have to agree with what Buchanan wrote in a letter to Richard Swedberg: "I foresee future development as blurring the distinctions between the social sciences generally, and not only between Economics and Sociology" (Swedberg 1990:4).

But the mingling of previously separate disciplines also brings about some phenomena like those mentioned by Swedberg (ibid., p.5) as the "trend of economists taking on traditional sociological topics - usually referred to as 'economic imperialism'". Later he explicates further: "One of the two disciplines can try to take over the subject matter of the other, which would constitute a case of 'economic imperialism' or 'sociological imperialism'" (ibid., p. 9) (cf. also Kalleberg 1995:1210-1213). But, as Swedberg (1990:322-323, 324) tells us on the basis of his interview series, in the "pecking order" of the social sciences economics has a higher status than sociology, and in consequence "economic imperialism" is much more frequent than the other way round. The somewhat pejorative meaning of the term "economic imperialism", a phrase, as Swedberg (ibid., p. 14) reveals, introduced by Souter "in the early 1930s", implies some hidden hostility or rivalry, and does not reflect the fact that various disciplines can greatly help one another. As Swedberg (ibid., p. 9) puts it: "A number of economists are realizing that many economic problems are extremely complex and cannot be solved with traditional economics alone."

Kalleberg (1995:1216) urges that "we should make it a priority to cross the boundaries between sociology and economics, so that we may enhance our understanding of both the economy and society". Baron and Hannan (1994), quoted with excellent taste by Swedberg (1996:xv), which I gratefully borrow now, are certainly right when they say that the "intrusion by economists and sociologists into one another's territory presents exciting opportunities for broadening each discipline and expanding interaction between them". Therefore it is both logical and justifiable that some sociologists, particularly White and Granovetter, as Swedberg (1990:7) tells us, "are of the conviction that the advances of the economists into traditional sociological areas should be met by a sociological counteroffensive, which shows that sociologists are not only capable of handling their traditional problems better than the economists, but that they can also help to solve several of the problems that the economists have failed to explain." He adds that "Granovetter feels that a 'new economic sociology' is about to emerge, whose distinguishing mark is precisely that it tries to tackle economic problems".

As Granovetter (1985b, reprinted in Granovetter and Swedberg 1992:76) himself says: "I believe the embeddedness argument to have very general applicability and to demonstrate not only that there is a place for sociologists in the study of economic life but that their perspective is urgently required there." The reason is, as Swedberg (1993a:59-60) opined at the end of a study of Schumpeter, that "neither economic theorists nor sociologists have the conceptual tools that would entitle them to an intellectual monopoly on economic phenomena".

Some scholars go even further, as Swedberg (1990:326-327) tells us after concluding his brilliant interview series. He reveals that Sen, White and Granovetter argue that "mainstream economics, as it exists today, cannot even solve its own problems". Granovetter is even more specific, stating that "... neoclassical economics cannot solve many of the problems within its own sphere of competence ..." (ibid., p. 327). Swedberg also points to Akerlof's "psycho-socio- and anthropo-economics", which claims that "economic theory by itself cannot explain some of the key problems in modern life; it needs the help of sociology and the other social sciences" (ibid., p. 336). Swedberg (1990:329) then reveals Coleman's view that "economics will one day become a subdiscipline of sociology".

Under these circumstances it is a logical consequence that a "new type of economic sociology" is evolving, which, according to Swedberg (1993b:xiv-xv), "is considerably more aggressive than its predecessors. It does not respect the economists' turf ...". Granovetter (1990:107) says in an interview with Swedberg about this new trend that "it is much less respectful of orthodox economics. 'New economic sociology' is much more ready to argue that sociologists have something to say about standard economic processes and that this supplements and in some cases also replaces what economic theory has to say." Later he adds that he sees no reason to be "so reluctant to explain economic phenomena in styles and modes of explanation that originate from other disciplines" (ibid., p. 111). Indeed, we should agree, it is entirely justified that, to use Swedberg's (1991:251) expression, "(t)his approach attempts to analyze core economic problems".

Obviously, the reason why I have quoted the views of prominent sociologists and economists in detail is that I am also "less respectful" "toward classical and neoclassical economic theory", to borrow the words of Granovetter (1990:107). In the same way as Granovetter (1985a), cited by Swedberg (1997:163), describes new economic sociology, namely that "it does not hesitate to attack neoclassical arguments in fundamental ways", I am actually taking on the currently still ruling orthodoxy: the main contemporary conservative trends in economics. These can be specified today as the standard monetarist and the New Classical, or, in other words, the "ultra-monetarist" creeds.

My basic message has as its starting point the fact that all modern, industrialized countries already have mixed economies today, as Sten Johansson (1994a:262) has revealed. As opposed to the prevalent conservative economic and political trends, the solution today cannot be found in illusions of a restoration of the pure market economy conditions of early 19th-century capitalism. On the contrary, the welfare characteristics of modern societies should be retained and even developed further, with prudent support given to the public sector. By public sector I mean what the Maastricht Treaty defines as being so (see here in a brief chapter on debt within the public sector); this was one of the minor matters well done in Maastricht, in contrast to other much greater issues.

This means that the public sector also includes all municipal, local administrations, hopefully with little bureaucracy and much direct democracy. Thus the public sector should not at all be disliked by those following ecological, "Green", "small is beautiful" trends, aptly denoted by Kitschelt and Hellemans (1990:5) as left-libertarian, and still possibly feeling some aversion towards the big "state", the big "government" (cf. Ahrne 1989:11-29 about bureaucracy, Ahrne 1998b:126 and Stephens 1996:36 about "statism"). The state, the government, should and indeed does transfer financial resources to the local communities. The question is how much. My suggestions involve giving more to the local levels because it is there that the bulk of welfare services are performed. Just as it is possible "to bridge the gap" between the "grand" and the "small" levels of research in the social sciences (cf. Hedström and Swedberg 1996, Hedström and Swedberg 1998a, Hedström and Swedberg 1998b; Hedström, Swedberg and Udéhn 1998:353; Ahrne and Hedström 1999:6), the same can be done in real life. Borrowing a few words from the title of a well-known work by Evans et al. (1985) we can say: "bring the public sector back in" to improve welfare services, health care and education.

As opposed to the currently fashionable conservative trends proposing the curtailment of the public sector, the task is to support it, and to develop the welfare state further by finding the "right" or "best" mix, or at least better mixtures of the mixed economy than exist today in modern countries. A more humane economy is needed, and this means more and better welfare services, less social inequality and less unemployment.

The solution that I suggest is 'combined Keynesian expansion' (CKE), which means increased direct public sector employment, preferably in welfare services, combined with monetary expansion. The latter is to be carried out by monetization, and without inflationary effects, because, depending on the flexible behaviour of central banks, the money supply is already endogenous in some important modern countries, wherever primarily the interest rates are kept regulated and fixed, for instance, in the United States.

As regards the theoretical background, monetarism and New Classical Macroeconomics are criticized, and a synthesis is proposed between New Keynesian and Post Keynesian trends.

In prosperous times some regular or constant wage-cost-push and demand-pull inflationary pressures may be generated as a result of the normal driving greed mainly within the private, market sector of the mixed economy, and to restrain these pressures the methods of comprehensive incomes agreements after centralized wage-talks and voluntary, organized consumer boycotts are suggested.

A terminological note: so far I have followed the "industrial society" tradition of theory and also denotations (cf. Erikson and Goldthorpe 1992:3-13; Kerr et al. 1960, Kerr 1983; Sollenius 1983, 1992). The descriptions of modern society as "service society" or "information society" certainly call attention to important current real characteristics; however, developed industrial technology stands behind all these changes as an inevitable precondition. On the other hand, the fundamental features of society, above all the core factor: the motivation system, have not changed. We still live in basically the same type of society. To use a very familiar, ideologically charged expression which by and large corresponds to "industrial society" used in my terminological framework: we still live in the same good old - or bad - "capitalism"; it has not been replaced, but has even grown stronger.

Without going into deeper theoretical reasonings at this point, I reconsider to some extent the term "industrial society" and regard it as modified to "industrialized society", in order to denote the advanced phase in which we all now live in the Western countries. So, the term WESTISM (Sollenius 1994) should be interpreted as modified accordingly. In this work I intend to use several adjectives synonymously to denote the contemporary Western type of society and countries, such as "industrialized", "advanced", "developed" and "modern".

To save the reader turning the pages backwards and forwards, I will again dispense with separate notes at the end of the book and, instead, will make detours by weaving the remarks into the main text.

To conclude this introduction, let me borrow and repeat an important thought from Swedberg's (1990:339) profound conclusion of his interview volume. He cites Amartya Sen's opinion, according to which economics and sociology are not so dissimilar because both disciplines "are about human life in society" and that "the ultimate concern has to be with the lives we can or cannot lead". Very much so. And this is why we should strive after constructing a more humane economy, I should like to add.

Stockholm, April 2000. J. S.

A POSSIBLE NEW CRISIS

THE PROMISING BOOM

The greatest world power of our days, the United States of America, undoubtedly takes up a central place in our Western political and economic life and in the related ideas, ways of thoughts. Even those Europeans who dislike extravagant American cultural influence have to admit grudgingly that today the U. S. should be considered the political and economic centre of the Western world and hence of our whole contemporary world. In consequence, the most characteristic feature for judging the economic state of affairs in the world is still the fairly long economic boom of the 1990s in the United States, despite the sluggish growth in some countries of Western Europe and a recent recession in Japan - to retain a "trilateral" way of thinking (cf. Sollenius 1983:15).

It has to be acknowledged that a boom took place in the United States through the 1990s, although statistics about dramatic, bright improvements in the jobs situation (cf., for instance, Council of Economic Advisers 1996) may have been somewhat misleading, as Martin and Schumann (1997:121-122) point out. Others, for.instance, a survey in the Le Monde Diplomatique quoted by Jacobsson (2000), even argue that in the statistics of the United States the high number of criminals in prison should be added to the number of unemployed, and then the latter would equal the European average.

But what creates today a confident mood and a great sense of euphoria among many economists in the United States, radiating optimism even to the stagnation or recession-stricken parts of our Western world, is the fact that "with the American economy seemingly triumphant", simultaneously "the stock market soared" and "Americans watched the stock market catapult upward", as Wolman and Colamosca (1997:197) put it. That is to say, the boom in the real economy was accompanied, at least up to October 1997, by a "relentless rise in the Dow" (ibid.). It was about seven years earlier, in October 1990, "when by common reckoning the current bull market began", according to Ip (1999). Naturally, there is a connection between the real economy and the stock market, but this relationship is assymmetrical as far as the time dimension is concerned. While the bourses can react immediately to any relevant or even less relevant news coming from the real economy, in the reverse direction the connection is not so close and rapid, since the real economy works much more slowly; it does not follow quick stock market moves, and it is influenced only by significant and somewhat lasting events or trends.

In October 1997, by and large 10 years after the 1987 autumn stock-market crash, something of a repetition of the 1987 events took place in the main stock exchanges of the world. This set-back broke the promising period of the uninterrupted mid-1990s boom in most Western bourses. Fortunately the baisse in the stock markets was left completely behind in a few months; the financial set-backs proved to be just temporary, something of a "correction" in hindsight, not causing any lasting recessions in the North-American and European countries. By early 1998 the stock markets seemed to be back to continuing the rise which had been uninterrupted in the preceding years, throughout the bulk of the decade.

And indeed, the figures of the Dow Jones index, perhaps the best indicator of business confidence in the United States and hence in the whole Western world, reached new heights in 1998. At the beginning of the year, when the index was still at about the 8000 level, but the Asian crisis seemed to have been overcome with the help of new IMF loans whose conditions the countries in trouble had grudgingly but finally accepted, optimistic forecasters said that the Dow Jones could be expected to recover "as it always does when a major crisis is over" and could reach the 8500 level. But in the hot summer the Dow surpassed even the 9000 level.

Then suddenly, from August 1998, the Russian economic crisis started to send shock-waves all around the globe and the stock exchanges of the world began to fall heavily again. By October all the index gains of 1998 had been wiped out on most money markets of the world and stock prices generally fell back below the level of the end of 1997. However, three interventions by the U. S. Federal Reserve, which decreased the federal funds rate by a mere one quarter of a percent each time, proved enough to restore confidence by about late 1998 and early 1999, when the Dow Jones returned to its summer 1998 levels.

In early 1999 a brief financial crisis in Brazil threatened the stability of the economies of the Latin American countries, a sensitive area for the United States, but a substantial IMF loan solved the situation, and after a brief panic the Dow started to rise again. Although in the spring of 1999 no one could prove that the movements of the Dow might have had any connection with the hard events of the Kosovo crisis, it is a simple fact that a few days after that resolute show of Western strength, the bombardment of Yugoslavia, starting on 24 March, the Dow Jones rose above the mark of 10,000, for the first time ever in its history, on 29 March 1999. At the end of April, while the bombing of Yugoslavia continued unabated, the Dow even went briefly over 11,000. After Yugoslavia gave in to the NATO demands in June the Dow soared again and by early July it exceeded 11,000 for a somewhat longer time.

During the summer of 1999 the Dow generally moved around 11,000, going above it several times. Only in late September did it start to dive again. But by the end of 1999 it hit new peaks and briefly surpassed the level of 11,500, finishing the year only 3 points below that. In January 2000 it even surpassed 11,700, returning to around 11,000 in February and around 10,000 in March.

The first main questions about the present situation might be: What is the basis of the boom of the 1990s? How long can and will it last? A second group of questions come as a counterpoint: What happened in the autumn of 1997 and in the autumn of 1998? Is that sequence of events definitely over? Or can it be repeated in the near or foreseeable future?

So, as regards the real economy of the United States, it continues to flourish. What factors can we thank for this long boom, which has now been is progress since late 1992?

The first main reason is in all likelihood political. In December 1991 the Soviet Union ceased to exist, breaking up into separate pieces entirely of its own accord. Its main successor state, Russia, plunged into a deep economic and political crisis, almost toppling over the borderline into complete dissolution itself. Hence the whole historical period of the Cold War, the threatening confrontation between what had sometimes been named "the two world-systems", was suddenly over. The great antagonist collapsed, dissolved, the United States remaining alone on the scene as the only superpower, the unchallenged leading country of the world. It seemed to be "the end of history", as Fukuyama (1989 and 1990) put it. A fundamental, lasting political euphoria came into being in the whole Western world, above all in the United States, and this has been nurturing business confidence powerfully ever since.

Another fundamental reason for the present economic boom in the United States and also in other advanced Western countries is technological. According to Krugman (1994:129), from about 1992 "something profound was taking place - a fundamental acceleration of productivity growth associated with new technologies applied in unexpected places". This development lies hidden in what, in Marxist and post-Marxist terminologies, used to be called "the forces of production" (cf. Sollenius 1983). Today it is most often identified closely with, as for instance Shepard (1997:48) puts it: "the revolution in information technology", often abbreviated as "IT". Indeed, information technology, as Shepard (ibid.) continues, "is all around us - fax machines, cellular phones, personal computers, modems, the Internet". It seems to play a similar role of "transcendent technology" in our days as railway building and the connected technology played in the 19th century and the automobile industry played throughout most of the 20th century (ibid., p. 49).

The service jobs connected with IT are of non-material character, and this is favourable from an ecological point of view. Information technology is developing dynamically indeed and has already become a significant job-creating industry in North America and Western Europe by the 1990s. However, its significance is often exaggerated deliberately by both fashion and a kind of market-oriented, so to say, "new capitalist" ideological zeal. As, for instance, Blix (1999) ironically writes: 'the whole world's hope is in IT in general and in the Internet in particular; have you noticed that Internet is spelt with capital letter like God?'

Shepard in fact first points to another decisive factor, which is a fundamental part of what he calls "the New Economy", of the positive trends "that have been under way for several years". This is "the globalization of business". He explains it as follows: "Simply put, capitalism is spreading around the world - if not full-blown capitalism, at least the introduction of market forces, freer trade, and widespread deregulation. It's happening in the former communist countries, in the developing world of Latin America and Asia, and even in the industrialized West - with economic union in Europe and North America's free-trade agreement. For the U.S., this means international trade and investment play a much greater role in our economic life than before. Twenty years ago, exports and imports made up 17 % of our economy. Today, they account for 25 %." (ibid.).

It is interesting to note, however, what Shepard, as well as some other contemporary authors, describe as a main or perhaps the most characteristic feature of our age: is not at all so new as it seems to be. Almost exactly 150 years ago two gentlemen whose names probably sound somewhat familiar but mostly disreputed to many leading contemporary economists, a Herr Marx and a Herr Engels, had already described the early phases of the same process in their "The Communist Manifesto", published in 1848 (cf. Elster 1986:225-234, especially 227-228, and 333).

Today, as we can see, the most recent phases of this long historical process are frequently summarized under the term "globalization". The details of this phenomenon are aptly analysed anew by Martin and Schumann (1997), who, in sharp contrast to

Shepard's (1997) view of the trend as an unmixed blessing, see a fundamental menace in the "global trap" and its accompanying features. According to the subtitle of their book, it is an "assault on democracy and prosperity".

"Global integration", Martin and Schumann (1997:8) say, "goes together with a doctrine of economic salvation ... The basic thesis, just a little simplified, is that the market is good and state intervention is bad ... Deregulation instead of state controls, liberalization of trade and capital movements, privatization of public enterprises" - these are the basic tenets of "a struggle for the freedom of capital that is still going on today", as they put it (ibid.). But the process is "building the dictatorship of the world market", they add, and this "'turbo-capitalism', which on a world scale now appears unstoppable, is destroying its own foundations as it undermines democratic stability and the state's ability to function" (ibid., p. 9).

THE POLITICAL FACTOR: RUSSIA

The main question today is how long the two most important reasons for the present boom - at least as far as the United States is concerned - the political and the technological, will last. The whole world is likely to follow the United States today in this respect.

The political factor ensuring a continued boom will in all likelihood last as long as Russia and the other successor states of the late Soviet empire remain in their present disintegrated way of existence both politically and economically. This only seems to be guaranteed as long as the leading group of the elite in Russia still believed to be broadly associated with the political heritage of ex-president Yeltsin remains in power. Yeltsin himself weathered several serious, critical moments of crisis after his ascension into the position of Russian president in the early summer of 1991, then still within the framework of the Soviet Union. His political survival was at first ensured in part by the logic of historical trends and in part by his own abilities, but later on more and more by the persistent Western support behind him. The latter was crucial for him, for instance, both in the form of media and public relations skills before the presidential election in the early summer of 1996, and in the form of the advanced technology of by-pass surgery curing his blocked heart arteries in the autumn of 1996, even if the operating surgeon himself was a Russian citizen. Naturally, the vast sums of Western financial support to Russia between 1992 and 1999 also played an important role in Yeltsin's favourable and comparatively long political survival.

Because of the undoubted influence of the Russian situation on the political and economic well-being of the United States and the whole Western world, it is perhaps not a waste of time if we dwell on the Russian story in some detail.

Ever since the dissolution of the one-time Soviet empire in late 1991 new phases in the prolonged economic crisis of Russia keep on developing. One of the latest chapters in this story started to appear in early 1998, despite some ostensible signs of partial economic improvements. By the first half of 1998 Russia succeeded in decreasing significantly its previously very high inflation rate, and, on the other hand, the shrinking of the total production figures of the Russian economy was estimated to have passed its bottom and the figures were expected to start to rise. Expectations focused on a measure of growth at long last, after the Russian GDP had fallen considerably during the previous years. Even today it can be assessed at only around half of what it was even in 1991, before the dissolution of the Soviet empire. The level of investments is still rather low as well, some analysts assessing it to be around a quarter of what it was in 1991. Nevertheless, before the beginning of 1998 it was hoped that the decreasing production levels would stabilize and start to rise again.

However, by about July 1998 it turned out that production levels were falling still further; in fact they fell about another 10 percent compared to the corresponding periods in 1997. The cost of the previous "stabilization" by means of strict monetary policy was a growing rate of unemployment and masses of wage arrears, salaries and wages unpaid for months, particularly within the public sector. Their sum was estimated to amount to 10 billion dollars. A basic cause of this phenomenon was the fact that state finances, and the collection of taxes in particular, were and are very weak in Russia even today. In addition, the decline in crude petroleum prices in the world in the first half of 1998 cut back the main export revenue of Russia considerably. By the summer of 1998 an acute crisis had developed in the Russian economy. The stock exchange started to fall and the

Russian rubel came under heavy pressure. The Kiriyenko government, appointed by Yeltsin only a few months earlier (after the March 1998 dismissal of the Chernomyrdin government, which had been in office during the previous five years), worked out an austerity package to satisfy the preconditions set by the IMF for providing emergency support to Russia.

Although the lower house of the Russian parliament, dominated by the communists, accepted only a smaller part of the austerity measures, a considerable part of the remaining gap in the state finances was nominally filled by means of presidential decrees and government regulations. The IMF acknowledged this Russian readiness to meet their conditions and started to transfer the first portion of a promised rescue loan of about 15 billion dollars in a year. Around late July the acute crisis seemed to be averted, but in August the Russian currency, the rubel, came under heavy pressure again. After spending the bulk of the first portion of the IMF rescue loan on the defence of the rubel, the Russian central bank gave in and the rubel was de facto devalued, beginning to drift downwards rapidly compared to the U.S. dollar. The stock market started to fall heavily, foreign investors began to move out from the Russian scene.

Probably under the influence of the Russian industrial oligarchy controlling the leading branches of the economy, which did not like Kiriyenko's efforts to subject them to the regular taxation discipline of the state, Yeltsin dismissed the merely few-month-old Kiriyenko government in the second half of August 1998 and called back Chernomyrdin to form a new emergency cabinet. But the lower house of the Russian parliament refused to accept him and this time Yeltsin backed down. In September he requested the veteran politician Primakov, the Minister of Foreign Affairs at that time, to form a new government. The lower house of parliament accepted Primakov in exchange for a promise to give the top position of minister responsible for economic affairs to a communist. Preparations started for introducing some restrictive measures in the economy, recalling memories of the state regulations of the past. Primakov announced brand new promises to pay off the vast sums of wage, salary and pension arrears that had been inflicting suffering on masses of

Russian public sector employees and pensioners for months. In early October the trade unions organized nation-wide strikes and protests in the country.

However, Primakov proved to be a very talented politician and succeeded in ensuring a period of relative stability, above all thanks to his efforts to pay off the arrears to the population, mainly by printing money and thus incurring the displeasure of the IMF. His popularity rose in the country and perhaps this led to Yeltsin's jealousy and/or some behind-the-scene intrigues against Primakov within the Russian political and economic elite, the various "clans", probably including the so-called "St. Petersburg group", and within that, among others, Putin. It is also possible that some sophisticated secret advice from Western political science experts suggested that Primakov's popularity should be saved from becoming worn off during the time left until the presidential election in 2000, and also to give him some anti-Yeltsin glamour of political 'martyrdom' in order to increase his chances in a possible decisive second round of the presidential election, where, it was perhaps supposed that time, he might stand against the communist leader Zjuganov.

No one knows the real reason, but the fact is that Yeltsin suddenly removed the popular Primakov on 12 May 1999 and in his place appointed Stepashin, another former leader of the secret service, just like one-time Primakov, and until then the head of the Ministry of the Interior in Primakov's government. A communist proposal in the lower house of the Russian parliament to impeach Yeltsin failed to get the necessary two thirds majority and subsequently the usually recalcitrant lower house accepted Stepashin and his government with unusual speed. This seemed to ensure a safe summer for the deputies, instead of a stormy period possibly caused by a threatening preliminary dissolution of parliament by Yeltsin.

Perhaps the Kosovo war also contributed to Primakov's fall. He went both to Yugoslavia and to NATO in order to mediate, but because he supported the Yugoslavian, that is, in fact the Serbian, side too much he failed to achieve a solution. After him the former prime minister Chernomyrdin made a new attempt at mediation, and in fact he helped to persuade Miloshevich to capitulate, even if formally not to NATO but to the United Nations, after his country suffered 78 days of heavy bombardment between 24 March and 10 June 1999. A few thousand Russian peace-keeping troops were also sent to Kosovo, but Chernomyrdin became a very unpopular politician in Russia, with any hopes for him in the presidential election in 2000 spoilt well in advance.

From August and September 1999 onwards shocking news began to emerge in the world press about the corruption and the maffia connections of the top Russian elite. Accusations included such crimes as the embezzlement of giant sums from the IMF loans to Russia, money laundering, accepting bribes, co-operating with the Russian maffia, etc. Investigations began at several places, for instance, at a construction firm in Switzerland (with an Albanian owner born in Kosovo) doing work in the Kremlin, and at The Bank of New York, among others. The rumours also deeply involved President Yeltsin and his family in the corrupt affairs, which the Russian investigators were quick to deny.

In early August 1999 Yeltsin suddenly removed Stepashin too and appointed Prime Minister a third former leader of the secret service, Putin; he also said that he saw in Putin his future successor as president. The lower house of the Russian parliament soon accepted Putin while Yeltsin announced that the next regular parliamentary election was to be on 19 December 1999. Putin's first tasks included the defence of the border regions of Dagestan from the attack and occupation by Chechen religious invaders, who also started their action in August. Despite the heavy deployment of Russian forces, it took five or six weeks to drive out the intruders from Dagestan. During the time of these battles Chechen terrorists blew up several apartment blocks in Dagestan, southern Russia and even in Moscow, with hundreds of innocent civilian dead and wounded. In reply, in addition to tight security measures throughout Russia, the Russian air force started a bombing campaign in late September against the Chechen country, to destroy the infrastructure and the economy in the same way as the NATO bombing campaign did in Yugoslavia in the spring of 1999.

At the beginning of October Russian land troops also crossed the border and started to invade the "bandit republic", as Prime Minister Putin called it, from several directions simultaneously. By the second half of December they occupied the bulk of the territory of Chechnya, except its capital, Grozny, which was encircled and under siege.

The person of Putin deserves specific attention, partly to compensate retrospectively for the almost universally belittling attitude in the world press that greeted his appointment by Yeltsin as Prime Minister and named successor in August 1999. At that time a British commentator said about Putin that he was the poor man's Stepashin, in other words, a stopgap of a stopgap, because Stepashin himself served as the head of the government for only about three months.

The most relevant information about Putin concerned his secret service background. Perhaps to some extent this explains his style of leadership, which can be characterized with the words: "act first, speak later". In contrast to the traditional attitude of many politicians who like delivering high-profile speeches, and who often consider the threat of an action as more effective and/or more useful than performing the action itself, Putin seems to be the man of action, even covert action. The course of the autumn 1999 phase of the recent Chechen war illustrates this fairly well. Before each stage the Russian political and military leadership carefully denied the planned escalation, the planned course of action, until the events were well under way or even almost completed. During the bombing campaign in late September they denied any intention of a land offensive, while concentrating considerable land forces around the borders of Chechnya. After the land invasion started, for a considerable period of time they still said that their only goal was to occupy limited territories and establish security zones along the borders. Only later, when a great part of Chechnya had already been occupied, was the real purpose of the war revealed, namely that this "bandit republic" had to be eliminated.

Putin turned out to be a very effective man, a man of deeds, a much more potent man than he was assessed to be at the time of his appointment. Thanks to the Chechen war Putin's popularity in Russia rose very quickly. After six weeks of the land war, by mid-November, he was already, according to the opinion polls, the most popular politician. Russian people had been outraged by the terrorists' bombing campaign in late August and early September claiming several hundred innocent civilian victims, and Russian nationalist feelings rose very high indeed in late 1999. Putin and the members of his government leading the Chechen war were seen as avenging heroes and the defenders of the Russian people.

No wonder that in the elections to the lower house of the Russian parliament, the Duma, on 19 December 1999 Putin's brand-new political party, emerging rapidly from nowhere, won a great many votes and finished as a very close runner-up behind the communists, who received about 24 percent of the votes. The nominal head of Putin's party was Shoygu, the Minister of Emergency Affairs in the government, who was seen and heard very frequently in the media as the organizer of the war effort. Putin's party took most of the votes from the party of Primakov and Luzhkov (the Mayor of Moscow), which received only about 12 percent of the votes and finished a poor third. Putin suddenly became the first favourite to win the presidential election, at that time still planned to take place in June 2000.

As regards the previous Chechen war, the speculation cannot be entirely excluded that it had been started in late 1994 in part with the intention of scoring some favourable points with the electorate before the parliamentary elections in 1995 and the presidential election in 1996. But that war was ill-timed and conducted catastrophically badly. It led to a counterproductive effect on Russian public opinion, mainly because of the high Russian casualty figures. In contrast, the Chechen war that started in the autumn of 1999 is seen by the Russian public as highly justified and it seems to be effectively conducted, with comparatively quick results and a limited number of Russian casualties. Although the victory did not come as early as it had been predicted by some officers, in early February 2000 the Russian troops finally succeeded in occupying Grozny and in the subsequent weeks they broke the main forces of the Chechen resistance even in the mountainous southern regions of the country. The remaining Chechen forces were reduced to guerilla warfare.

Prime Minister Putin became very popular and he gained a good chance of becoming the next president of Russia. A likely scenario was that he receives more than fifty percent of all votes in the first round of the presidential election, just as Yeltsin did in 1991; or he may defeat the communist leader, Zjuganov, the most likely runner-up, in the second round, just as Yeltsin did in 1996.

On the last day of 1999 Yeltsin suddenly resigned and Putin became the acting head of state in addition to being Prime Minister. This new situation greatly enhanced his chances of winning the presidential election, which became then scheduled a few months earlier, the first round already in late March. Some observers suspect a silent coup in the background of the events, together with a bargain. Putin immediately granted ex-president Yeltsin, who was from that time onwards tactfully called "the first president of Russia", as well as his family-members, complete immunity from any kind of investigation, including possible corruption charges. Nevertheless, Putin instantly removed Yeltsin's daughter from her position as presidential adviser. He obviously jettisoned her as a potential liability.

As expected, Putin did win the presidential election already in the first round on March 26, even if with a slightly smaller margin than it had been predicted by the opinion polls; he received an absolute majority: about 52 and a half percent of all votes. The communist leader, Zjuganov, was the runner-up with about 30 percent, and adding to this the votes received by another, less known and more left-wing communist candidate, it turned out that about one third of the electorate still favoured the communists.

Many Western politicians and observers hailed Putin's likely victory in advance and hoped that the Western influence in Russia will continue unchanged. However, Putin is not Yeltsin and after ascending to power now he might choose a different course of policies, a more nationalist line. His hard attitudes may already be judged by the Chechen war. As early as the last quarter of 1999 Russia's relationship to the West became considerably cooler, due mainly to Western complaints about the indiscriminate and disproportionate shelling of towns and villages in Chechnya, the cruel character of the whole Russian conduct of the war, which resulted in enormous suffering for the innocent civilian population in the war zone. Putin's government rejected Western efforts to try to start mediation between the Russians and the Chechen leaders, the Russian standpoint being that no negotiations can take place as long as the Chechen leaders fail to condemn the terrorists among their countrymen. Anyway, said Putin's government, the elected Chechen leaders no longer had any real power, because the local terrorist warlords had taken over real control. Terrorists of any kind should in general be combated harshly, and Islamic terrorists of the same or similar brand that recently blew up two embassies of the United States in Africa and caused hundreds of dead and wounded should in particular be combated harshly, Putin's Russian government argued, more or less logically.

The cooler relationship on the basis of the Chechen war may be only a faint early signal of the kind of unpleasant surprise the West might experience now, after Putin and his team have gained full control of Russia. Putin, the effective earlier secret service leader, might start to put into practice some policies that are quite different from those he had to follow under Yeltsin's time. One clue in this respect might be the fact that in the 19 December 1999 parliamentary election the real "zapadniki", that is, the real followers of the West, politicians like Gaydar, Chubays and Nemtsov, did not join Putin's party but formed a separate party under the leadership of the young former reformist prime minister Kiriyenko. They did surprisingly well, not only getting into the Duma above the five percent limit against all the odds, but, with about 9 percent of the votes, finishing as the fourth largest party.

Perhaps a few additional clues can be found in a BBC interview in March, where Putin said, among others, that in contrast with Yeltsin he intends to pursue policies that Russian people need and want. In a last major statement before the first round of the presidential election o, Putin said that a completely new era would begin for Russia, reminding the audience that his country is a great nuclear power, whose president is simultaneously the supreme commander of the armed forces, and he emphasized the need to restore Russia's international authority and leading role in the world. It is not likely that this politician is going to continue Yeltsin's sometimes grandiloquent but in practice fairly obedient and humble attitude towards the West.

President elect Putin is already very active and he might even intend to influence in advance the outcome of the presidential election in the United States this autumn. Indeed, Russia may probably hope to get more economic support from a future Democrat administration than from a Republican one, even indirectly, through international institutions, and apart from that, in general terms, Russia might prefer a liberal American president to a dye-hard Republican. This fact might have played a role in the event that only about a week after the official announcement of the final results of the Russian presidential election Putin scored another quick victory over his communist rival, Zjuganov. In mid-April both houses of the Russian parliament suddenly ratified the START-2 treaty between the U.S. and Russia about the mutual decrease and limitation of the number of all kinds of strategic nuclear warheads. This treaty had been waiting for the Russian ratification ever since 1993, and Putin's quick success with it has greatly contributed to the progress of nuclear disarmament. Clinton and Putin have already agreed to meet in Moscow in July to continue the process of strategic arms reduction still further. In the second half of April the Russian parliament also ratified the nuclear test ban treaty, which has not yet been ratified even by the U.S. Congress. These Russian developments are very good news indeed for the whole population of the Earth.

However, a few days after the favourable vote on the nuclear test ban treaty in the Duma, the lower house of parliament, Putin signed a new Russian military doctrine, which makes it easier to deploy nuclear weapons in defence of Russia in a conflict. Only a day or two before the ratification of START-2 in the Duma, Putin appointed a new chief economic adviser, Illarionov, who immediately announced his view that Russia should stop accepting IMF loans. About a week later Putin ordered his National Security Council to increase Russian economic (and inevitably also political) presence vigorously in the oil-rich region of the Kaspian Sea, to confront American, British and Turkish aspirations. No doubt these developments carry the signs of Putin's nationalist intentions to restore Russia's great power positions and pride.

Mixed signals are coming from President elect Putin just a couple of weeks before his installation, due in early May 2000, and only time will tell the exact traits of his ultimate political agenda. Might his future rule develop a kind of historical mixture between the "revolutionary intellectuals" and the "nationalist leader" types of industrialization distinguished by Kerr et al. (1960) and Sollenius (1983, cf. also 1992:36-37, in particular), while also converging towards the Western model?

According to the opinion of George Soros, the well-known economic expert with an East European descent, Putin is going to prove an authoritarian and nationalist leader, and no further development of democratic political and economic reforms can be expected now in Russia. His judgement is in all likelihood correct. Some Russian experts warn that to satisfy the overwhelming desire of Russian people to do away with the present chaos and lawlessness, Putin's rule is going to bring a kind of "dictatorship of the law". In other words, Putin will try to increase the authority of the state and impose order and discipline everywhere in a heavy-handed way.

Some minor but characteristic events might also help to know more about Putin's attitudes and sympathies. Not long before the presidential election he paid tribute to the late Andropov, a prominent one-time head of the KGB, the Soviet secret service, who had also played a role in the suppression of the 1956 Hungarian uprising, being ambassador in Hungary at that time. In an interview Putin casually mentioned that he is still on good terms with the retired Kryuchkov, the head of the KGB in 1991, who is known to have been the chief mastermind of the failed August 1991 coup against Gorbachov. Putin is said to have spent his first evening after his victory in the presidential election at an anniversary festival of the troops of the Ministry of the Interior. In January 2000 Putin's party struck a deal with the communists about the distribution of leading positions in the Duma, the lower house of the Russian parliament, and as a result the communists obtained the position of the Chairman of the Duma together with the chairmanship of the nine most important committees.

For that matter, Putin's party has nominally been led by Shoygu, who is said to be a great enthusiast of the former Soviet Union. After pacifying and in practice reintegrating Chechnya into Russia, President Putin is by no means sure to be able to resist the temptation of drifting on towards an even more nationalist political course and trying to reintegrate the whole former empire in one form or another. Had the communist leader Zjuganov won the presidential election, the trend of reintegration concerning the whole empire would have got the upper hand automatically. But such a course of policy might also ensue under President Putin.

Yeltsin's presence in the presidential post was crucial for the the development of democracy in Russia and the yet unfinished transformation of the economy along market lines. He was the key man for the West. After he left the scene it is not at all sure now that a politician with a similar attitude towards the present disintegrated conditions within the former empire has stepped into his place.

Yeltsin was the mastermind of the political dissolution of the Soviet Union in early December 1991. It was only Yeltsin among the leading Russian politicians who gained his top position by playing the disintegration card. This was his great scheme for ascending to power. Consequently this policy was not to be reversed as long as he sat in the saddle, in spite of any lip-service to the connections between the successor states of the late Soviet empire. But most of his possible successors in secret had in all likelihood more positive attitudes towards a contingent reintegration of the successor states in one form or another. Since the disintegration process was closely associated with Yeltsin's person alone, after his departure a general mood of reintegration might evolve, from which perhaps not even President Putin might be able to keep himself apart, in addition to his yet unknown personal attitude to this question.

The possibility of a revived Russian empire thus cannot be excluded, this is all the more so because in effect no military conflicts would be necessary for a reintegration. It happened to be an extreme nationalist who first revealed the fact that sheer economic pressure may well be enough to force through a reintegration. Most of the successor states are heavily dependent on Russian raw material and energy resources. In consequence a possible reintegration might be much easier than most Western experts believe. If the three Slavic states: Russia, the Ukraine and Belorussia, which had formed the core of the one-time Soviet empire, happen to reunite, then most of the other nine states of the twelve present members of the Commonwealth of Independent States may follow suit comparatively quickly. Of the one time fifteen republics of the former Soviet Union the three Baltic states are not members of the present Commonwealth, and they are likely to remain apart from a possible process of reintegration.

Among the three Slavic states in the centre of the one-time empire, the small Belorussia is now under the leadership of a kind of post-communist dictator, Lukashenko, and he has already shown himself willing or even eager to reunite his country with Russia. In December 1999 a new treaty about this was again signed by Yeltsin and Lukashenko, not for the first time, and some malicious observers even suspected on Yeltsin's part a hidden motive of trying to find a pretext to prolong his presidency in the last hour in some way, by referring to this new formation of states. The treaty was then quickly ratified by the Russian parliament, but it only established a very loose confederation and has merely symbolic significance today.

The most relevant question, in effect the key question concerning the whole process of reintegration is the behaviour of the Ukraine. Perhaps it is not an exaggeration to assert that just as the disintegration of the Soviet empire in December 1991 was in reality decided by a plebiscite in the Ukraine, a possible reunification of the empire would also be decided by the behaviour of the Ukraine. And the Ukraine is heavily dependent on Russia economically, in particular on Russian energy resources, above all crude oil. Besides that, in the eastern parts of the Ukraine there is a large Russian minority population. Serious political confrontation might develop between the eastern and the western regions of the Ukraine on a possible "reunion with Russia" issue, and the eastern parts, perhaps with forceful Russian support, might finally overcome the reluctant, independent-minded Westerners. A possible reintegration of first the three Slavic states under discussion and later the others might even be arranged in an artful way, with some nominal autonomy kept: independent flags, coats-of-arms, anthems, presidential titles and other prestigious requisites preserved to satisfy national and individual vanities. Such a process might even be launched by nominally keeping the present name of the Commonwealth of Independent

States, but under the economic pressure of a more nationalist-minded Russia gradually making it more and more integrated.

A process of reintegration of the empire cannot be excluded, and that would be disadvantageous from the viewpoint of Western political interests, in particular those of the United States. The historical period of our more or less undisturbed Western political euphoria since 1991 or already since 1989, the fall of the East European satellite regimes, might hence come to an end as early as the first decade of the new millenium. Even if not a new Cold War but something of a Cool or Cold Peace might develop again on the basis of great power rivalry. No doubt, an unfavourable political turn in Russia would also seriously influence the fate of the economic trends in the advanced West, both in the short and the long run, particularly in Europe. Similar to the economic setbacks starting in August 1998, but on a bigger scale, a serious recession might ensue in Europe. As for the United States, the effects might be similar in the beginning, but if a new arms race evolved with a reunited and again ambitious old-new Russian empire, then it would probably give a forceful new impetus to economic demand in the U. S. later, in the long run.

A NEW RECESSION?

The question can be raised whether, even apart from the political factor of the Russian situation, the economic trends described in the United States in particular and in the whole Western world in general really are so triumphant, victorious as they seemed to be during most of the 1990s.

In general, the world-wide process of 'globalization' is not going ahead at all so smoothly and victoriously as it was hoped by many. A conspicuous illustration of this fact was the utter failure of the WTO conference in Seattle between 30 November and 3 December 1999. Characteristic of the obstacles was in particular the resounding collapse of the talks on a "Multilateral Agreement on Investment", MAI, which was to have been driven through in order to subordinate national governments to the will of globalizing capital, the multinational corporations. Hence the future remained uncertain foran important objective in the game of globalization: the possibilities for the "multis" to appropriate the bulk of the extra profit created by the transfer of production processes to underdeveloped, developing countries with very cheap labour, low taxes and low social costs.

As regards the glory of a symbolic flagship of the contemporary processes mentioned, the stock-exchange and the rising of the Dow Jones Industrial Average to new and new heights, there are some sceptical opinions about them as well. Some people see them as a kind of collective upwriting, that is, merely as upbidding games of the subjective value of equities in the stock market. In Korten's (1995:190) opinion "(t)here are two common ways of creating money without creating value. One is by creating debt. Another is by bidding up asset values. The global financial system is adept at using both of these devices to create money delinked from the creation of value." As regards stock assets, Korten (ibid., p. 191) explains that "demand is substantially influenced by speculators' expectation that other speculators will continue to push up the price." Then "(a)s the price of an asset rises, more speculators are drawn to the action and the price continues to increase, attracting still more speculators - until the bubble bursts..."

The result of the world-wide process of "deregulation" of financial systems since the early 1980s, also allowing various kinds of financial activities to mingle under one roof, has been the development of giant all-round financial empires, engaged in vast speculative activities. As Korten (1995:192, 193) reveals: "What we are dealing with is a situation in which market speculation creates an illusion of wealth. ... The global financial system has become a parasitic predator that lives off the flesh of its host - the productive economy." Or to put it even more exactly, "(f)inancial institutions that were once dedicated to mobilizing funds for productive investment have transmogrified into a predatory, risk-creating, speculation-driven global financial system engaged in the unproductive extraction of wealth from taxpayers and the productive economy" (ibid., p. 205). Korten's prediction is ominous: "This system is inherently unstable and is spiraling out of control - spreading economic, social, and environmental devastation and endangering the well-being of every person in the planet." (ibid., p. 206).

Chancellor (1999) reveals the striking similarity between the stirring, highly optimistic financial activities of the 1920s prior to the Great Depression and the great boom in the bourses of the world in our days, around the turn of the millenium.

Martin and Schumann (1997:88-95) vividly describe the high degree of vulnerability of our world's new, globalized financial system, which has developed enormous bubbles of speculation, especially through the highly risky derivatives, far transcending any connections with the real economy. "The explosion of the derivatives trade has not only increased the risks for the money business, but also disabled security systems in the financial sector that took decades to put in place", they write (ibid., p. 88). In consequence "danger threatens the whole system...when big banks and investment firms become insolvent. The plight of one institution can affect others overnight and trigger a worldwide domino effect. 'Then the risk spills over to the exchanges, from there to the exchange rates and so into the real world'... Such a mega-disaster is 'altogether possible'. Trade would suddenly come to a stop, the whole system would collapse, and a global crash as on Black Friday, October 1929, would be unavoidable", warn Martin and Schumann (ibid., p. 89).

Fortunately, today we are not (yet) facing such a harsh scenario, but some ominous signs of a possible new economic recession might already be discerned.

One source of possible threatening future developments is the fact that the series of unfavourable economic events generally summed up today under the heading of the "Asian crisis" seems not to be completely over yet. A number of South-East Asian countries have had serious economic difficulties since about 1997. After numerous years of rapid economic growth a measure of relative deceleration followed; it then turned out that most investors in these so-called "tiger economies" had for years heavily overestimated the general pace of development in this region. The belief in everlasting, high-speed growth turned out to be unrealistic, and this galling truth materialized in masses of bad loans leading to financial crises in several countries.

Some observers believe that the event which triggered the 1997 Asian recessions was basically political: the historical return of Hong Kong to mainland China on 1 July 1997. This may well have been the case as regards an initial push, but the deeper reasons, the background of the "Asian crisis", probably lie hidden in the feudalistic vestiges of these societies, the characteristic features of those types of industrialization processes which were originally initiated and led by either the "colonial administrators", as in most countries of the region, or by the "dynastic elite", as in the leading Asian economy, Japan, according to Sollenius (1983), following the typology of Kerr et al. (1960). Feudalistic nepotism and cronyism (cf. Editorial 1997a, Editorial 1997b) greatly contributed or definitely caused the accumulation of vast sums of never repayable, bad investment loans, also based on hopes of continued high-speed, extensive growth, as mentioned. Sooner or later the day of financial reckoning in these countries had to come, and a considerable part of it might still be to come.

The acute financial crisis in Hong Kong was temporarily averted in late 1997 with the backing of the big new-old motherland, mainland China, but the crisis swept through most South-East Asian economies. And when the Asian recession began seriously to affect the leading economy and the main banker of the region, Japan, which had loaned vast sums throughout these countries, and which, on the other hand, also has strong connections with the economy of the United States, the course of events started to turn serious indeed. The stock-market setbacks around the globe in October 1997 came as the result of a sudden wave of panic caused by the first great quake of the Asian crisis.

Nevertheless, with the help of great sums of IMF support to several Asian countries, above all to Indonesia, South Korea and Japan, and also with some political change here and there, above all the replacement of the old dictator, Suharto, in Indonesia, the Asian crisis was successfully contained during 1998 and 1999. Or at least it seems so, because this time of relief might prove to be only a temporary breathing space. In 1999 Indonesia granted independence to East Timor, after a referendum and subsequent bloody massacres there by local armed militias loyal to Indonesia. Since then tensions threatening to break up the vast Indonesian state have also occurred in other regions.

In Japan the recession has started to be gradually mitigated thanks to some typical Keynesian measures of state interference: subsidies, state guarantees, some public works programs and above all the setting up of huge funds by the government to support the reorganization of the banking sector. The value of the Yen has improved but the financial sector continues to be burdened by bad loans. Should the Japanese crisis happen to deepen again, at least 100 billion dollars of Japanese-owned United States government securities might be submitted to the U. S. Treasury through mediating agencies, in order to be redeemed instantly. This could cause some disturbance in the U.S. economy as well, although paradoxically such an effect can be mitigated by the contingent evolution of some renewed crisis symptoms in the 'developing markets' of other parts of the world, above all in Russia and Latin America. Namely, fleeing capital from these regions may come home to the West, and if stock-markets there start to fall again, such capital may find a haven in safe U. S. government bonds and buy them in great numbers. As regards Western stock-exchanges in general, renewed crises in Russia, Asia and even possibly Latin America might prove to be contagious again.

What seems to be common to both the almost permanent Russian crisis and the recent and possibly reappearing Asian crisis is the ominous fact that the possibilities of external help might gradually be diminishing in the future. The IMF offered generous loans in late 1997 and in 1998 to several countries in deep trouble, in particular Indonesia, South Korea and Japan, even up to about 40 or 50 billion dollars, but the severe conditions attached to the rescue, although accepted on paper, may often prove too hard to be met in practice by the recipient countries. In addition and above all, even these huge sums of support might prove to be insufficient to put all the recipient countries swiftly back in order, despite the fact that, for instance, the Japanese crisis showed some remarkable signs of recovery in 1999, after the setting up of huge public funds to support the reorganization of the banking sector.

As regards the external economic aspects of the Russian situation, the IMF seems ready to provide support here too from time to time, but it may prove difficult to drive through the harsh conditions attached to the loans even in the recently elected lower house of the Russian parliament. What is still more important, these loans with the considerable size of 12 to 15 billion dollars annually are in effect peanuts compared to the huge amounts of missing money needed by Russia to prop up and restore its economy. The sums at issue offered by the

IMF for a whole year, attached to strict preconditions of tight monetary policy, could well prove to be merely enough for a month or two. Russia seems to be a bottomless barrel.

So, the size of both the Russian and the Asian crises, if they are possibly renewed and superimposed on each other, may dwarf possible IMF loans rapidly. And the IMF is often near the end of its lending capacity in these years; from time to time it seems to be scratching the bottom of its coffers. The chances that this source may soon be replenished generously, for example, by the United States, are meagre. At any rate, replenishment with those vast sums that might be needed for Russia and Asia is probably out of the question.

Unfortunately, even the economy of the United States may be vulnerable, despite the quick recovery of the stock exchange in late 1998 and the continuation of the boom in 1999. According to Godley (1999), there had developed in the United States by the late 1990s an unprecedented decline in the private sector financial balance. As he says, "(t)he expansion of the US economy since 1992 has depended on the growth of net lending to the private sector; and it is on the continued growth of that lending that the further expansion of the economy must now depend, given that the budget is in surplus and trade is in deficit". His projections "suggest that if the private balance were to revert to its normal level between now and 2003 ... the economy would more or less stop growing, with the average growth rate barely positive over the next five years as whole. The budget surplus would also disappear and unemployment would rise to 7 per cent or more." He adds that "(t)he most pronounced effects (of the impact) would be in Latin America and Asia which would suffer a fresh round of substantial deflationary shocks". He concludes that although "the US boom may well continue for several more quarters ... there are major perils ahead and policy will need to be substantially changed ...". He expresses his belief that "change will involve a full scale rehabilitation of fiscal policy worldwide and that the ideas that underlie macroeconomic policy will have to be revised according to Keynesian principles".

Returning to the topic of information technology, let us insert now a somewhat futuristic note. It may be supposed that in the more distant future the universal spreading of computerization might considerably reduce the use of money itself and hence the role of monetary policy in economic life. The age of calculation and planning with real quantities, "in kind", might arrive, with the possible use of working-time units. The using of such money-free calculations might perhaps also reduce the occurrence and seriousness of the phenomenon of inflation. A kind of more "money-free" economy might become more "inflation-free" as well.

As regards a shorter, more prosaic time perspective, information technology in the advanced Western countries in general and the United States in particular may continue to sustain some kind of a boom for several more years, but in the first decade of the new millenium its products will probably approach saturation in several West-European and North-American countries. For instance, in the leading IT country: Sweden, according to Lignell (2000a), half of the population already used the Internet in early 2000, and the number of cellular phone subscriptions by late 2000 may well exceed 7 million within a population of somewhat under 9 million (cf. Metro 2000a, 2000b, 2000c). After about 75 or 80 percent of households or persons have been supplied with contemporary IT products, further sales of such items may slow down. This may be a process similar to that concerning automobiles in the recent decades of the 20th century. Information technology may still produce more and more sophisticated inventions for prestige consumption or prestige accumulation, but the time of the very rapid spread of new IT articles will probably come to an end in the most advanced countries in a decade or even sooner.

The reason is that the use of these articles in everyday life has obvious, natural time-limits for human beings. Many people who have them today are already fed up with being inundated with faxes, e-mails, cellular phone-calls, TV-channels (cf. Sundelin 1999, Nordvall 2000 and Lignell 2000b). The great IT playroom may become filled at least as much as the automobile market had become earlier. People's capacity to play with IT toys is limited. They may easily become bored. It does not really matter if one has 20 television channels or 200, one cannot enjoy more than a tiny fragment of all those programs. Embarras de richesse. (Let alone the deteriorating cultural quality of most programs: soap-operas, sci-fi, action, crime, thriller, horror, all rather primitive stuff.) The truth is that IT does not satisfy basic human needs; apart from being a very useful everyday working tool indeed, it serves only as an extra pastime at leisure, an at first interesting but later less and less interesting toy.

After some years saturation may well cause the end of the period of very rapid, dynamic growth of production of new IT articles. IT will probably become just another branch of industry and services, exposed to the capricious changes of boom and slump. We say services too, because in addition to the production of IT equipment this is also true of the large number of service jobs connected with information technology: programmers, consultants, instructors, repairers, etc. These jobs will also reach a saturation phase and the current rapid increase of their numbers will slow down. They will become just another kind of service job with hiring and firing as usual. For that matter, although the current development of IT does give new toys and new games to society with a number of new jobs to the labour market, it also rationalizes out many old jobs (for instance, in office work, retailing trade, etc.), and, according to Källberg (2000), it only creates one new job for three old jobs destroyed.

As regards the future of the boom of the 1990s in (some parts of) the West in general and in the United States in particular, the combined political and economic effects of a few crises in the world possibly evolving anew in the early 2000s: a culminating, "reintegration" phase of the almost permanent Russian crisis, a possibly renewed Asian crisis, and perhaps a new crisis in the rather volatile backyard of the United States, Latin America, may work much more rapidly than any saturation in the domain of IT. Such effects may elicit a new world recession or at least a serious stagnation already in a year or two, perhaps even sooner, and at any rate far sooner than the inherent growth capacities of the IT industries and services can run their natural course.

Hobsbawm (1996:584-585) writes that "there are signs, both externally, and, as it were, internally, that we have reached a point of historic crisis. The forces generated by the techno-scientific economy are now great enough to destroy the environment, that is to say, the material foundations of human life. The structures of human societies themselves, including even some of the social foundations of the capitalist economy, are on the point of being destroyed by the erosion of what we have inherited from the human past. Our world risks both explosion and implosion. It must change. ... And the price of failure, that is to say, the alternative to a changed society, is darkness."

TOWARDS A SOLUTION

PRACTICAL ELEMENTS OF SYNTHESES

While the economy of the United States was having its ups and downs during the last few decades, interesting developments took place in economic theory. A thorough and vivid account of the struggle between Keynesian ideas in alliance with liberal political trends on the one side and monetarist as well as rational expectationist ideas in alliance with conservative political forces on the other side is given, for instance, by Krugman (1994:23-54). Nevertheless, as regards the contemporary state of this age-old theoretical struggle, Krugman's (ibid., pp. 17, 197-220) conclusion seems to be somewhat too optimistic, I think. "By 1992, monetarist and rational expectations theorists had lost virtually all influence over actual policy, in the United States and elsewhere", the otherwise excellent Krugman evidently believes (ibid., pp. 197-198); yet this statement seems to be a little hurried and exaggerated. He possibly feels this to some extent himself when he simply puts the blame on the press for the fact that the public has not yet taken notice of the "rebirth of Keynesian economics" (ibid., p. 198). It "has been oddly ignored by the press,...reporting on macroeconomics often seems locked in a time warp" - he says (ibid.). "I'm not sure why the real story hasn't gotten out" - he admits and concludes that "it may simply be that the revival of Keynesianism has not had the kind of obviously colorful characters that make for entertaining stories" (ibid.).

I can readily agree with Krugman's (ibid.) main point that "in the long run it seems that Keynes is still alive - and it is his critics who seem to lack staying power", but I feel that at present it is still the conservative trends in macroeconomics that are in power, overwhelmingly influencing economic and political decisions in most Western countries as well as in international organizations like the EU, the IMF, the World Bank, and the WTO. The followers of new Keynesian macroeconomics, though hopefully and in all likelihood in the ascendant, as Krugman optimistically asserts, are at present still in a meagre minority, both in (at least the European) academic circles and in the citadels of real power. There is a great amount of intellectual work to be done before the situation changes in the way that Krugman forcefully but a little too hastily anticipates.

Nevertheless, there is, no doubt, a promising development in connection with the "rebirth of Keynesian economics" described and greeted by Krugman, and this is the spreading application of economic practice involving some kinds of syntheses between Keynesian and monetarist macroeconomic principles. In fact the fairly successful work being done by the Chairman of the Federal Reserve System of the United States, de facto the head of the central bank of the U. S., and by the Federal Open Market Committee (FOMC), which includes the Board of Governors of the "Fed", is a good example. Their activity in carefully regulating the development of the giant economy of the United States throughout the 1980s and particularly in the 1990s is a good example of the kind of synthesis mentioned above or at least a trend toward it. This becomes obvious in the characterization of this regulating process by Jones (1994), Leonard (1994), Sternlight (1994) and Daane (1994), in Colander and Daane (1994). As these authors point out, the process of directing the economy of the United States is based on accumulated long-time experience and consists of little movements of correction whenever some interference seems necessary.

According to Jones (1994:86-87): "The FOMC's primary policy guidelines are...the federal funds rate and depository institutions' borrowings at the Fed discount window. The federal funds rate is the rate on bank reserve balances at the Fed that are loaned and borrowed among banks, usually overnight." Later he explains: "...borrowed reserves are a very small piece of total reserves...Even though borrowings are an infinitesimal part of the reserves total, they are the most sensitive indicator of Fed-induced changes in reserve pressures. The Fed has joint operating guidelines of the Fed funds rate and borrowed reserves. To predict interest rates, one must watch how the Fed intervenes in the market in order to influence this Fed funds rate." (ibid., p. 96).

As Jones (ibid., p. 95) also reveals, "from 1979 to 1982 the Fed targeted the supply of nonborrowed reserves", that is to say, the great bulk of all bank reserves, the most essential part of the monetary base, in a modish monetarist creed of the time, we can add. Krugman's assertion that a Keynesian revival has already arrived seems to have come true at least at the Fed, which today no longer puts emphasis on nonborrowed reserves, but instead, "since 1987...has focused on twin operating guidelines: borrowings and the Fed funds rate" (ibid.), of which the latter represents a Keynesian attention paid to the importance of interest rates.

Now the Fed's open market operations, usually one-day repurchase agreements (RPs), mostly aim at influencing the federal funds rate, which "represents the primary cost of short-term loanable funds" and whose changes "will influence the prime bank lending rate...Changing these interest rates will then affect aggregate demand" throughout the country (ibid., p. 99). Even relatively small measures of intervention by the Fed are enough, they work properly, because they can "communicate its policy intentions" to "the financial markets" (ibid., p. 96).

As regards the theoretical background of this practice, Jones (1994:99) says that behind the Fed's method of regulation there is "a modified Keynesian aggregate demand model in which real output responds to shifts in demand". He also reveals that "the Fed's use of the yield curve (or the spread between short and long-term interest rates) as an intermediate policy indicator is grounded in neo-Wicksellian theory" (ibid., p. 91). Nevertheless, the practical movements of regulation are not based on any precise, exact theoretical calculation. This is why the editors gave the book the title: "The Art of Monetary Policy", with Jones (1994:85) putting it explicitly: "Economic policymaking is an art, not a science."

In fact the regulatory work of the Fed is the practical materialization of what economists of the orthodox monetarist creed often referred to ironically as an illusory Keynesian aim of "fine tuning". The process is in fact a kind of fine tuning or at least a serious attempt at it, based on practical knowledge and experience. It is characteristic that among the members of the Federal Open Market Committee there are indeed various shades of both the Keynesian and the monetarist schools of economics. Leonard (1994), for instance, admits and explains his monetarist conviction. As Jones (1994:100) remarks about the above mentioned Keynesian theoretical background: "Not everyone accepts this story. The monetarists on the Fed Board say it is all wrong. Just hit a monetary target." And he adds: "...there seem to be nearly as many theories of how policy interacts with the economy as there are members of the FOMC. But...in the end, Fed officials must agree on actual policy decisions to deal with the actual economic world."

What the Fed does in practice is a pragmatist compromise between Keynesianism and monetarism. On the one hand, it manifests itself in the fact that while paying primary attention to the federal funds rate, the Fed also watches and sets target ranges for monetary and credit aggregates. On the other hand, it is a compromise between and a fine mixture of what is usually called activism or discretionism, being mainly on the Keynesian side, and what is usually called rulism, being mainly on the monetarist side of the great theoretical frontline in economics during the latest decades. In a passage with the title "Rules versus Discretion" Sternlight (1994:110) says about Fed operations: "A recurring theme ... is the degree of discretion to be allowed in implementing policy ... as opposed ... to pursuit of some sort of fixed rule such as a money supply or growth target. The tradition at the Fed's trading desk is to favor a sizable dollop of discretion ... The search or hunger for rules has tended to come more from the academic world, perhaps because some people in that quarter have a natural distrust of the foibles of merely human practitioners."

He continues: "My problem with rigid rules ... is that relationships can and do change in a dynamic economy ...". Then Sternlight adds: "On the other hand, total 'discretion' is not a totally satisfactory answer either. There have to be principles guiding that discretion and, hopefully, some capable people to exercise it." (ibid., p. 111).

A good summary of such confrontations of these main principles is also given, for instance, by Dornbusch and Fischer (1990:463-466). As they point out, the notion of discretionism is somewhat more particularistic than the notion of activism, because even activist rules can be invented (ibid., pp. 463-465). In practice, however, a monetarist rule of the classical sort given by Milton Friedman (1968:16), which says: "something like a 3 to 5 percent per year rate of growth in currency plus all commercial bank deposits or a slightly lower rate of growth in currency plus demand deposits only", obviously cannot be kept sharply, with any precision; it can only be kept by and large, approached roughly. This is why, as Dornbusch and Fischer (1990:419) describe, a central bank, for example, the Fed, can set target ranges for the money and credit supply growth, that is, ranges for M2, M3 and debt growth, as well as ranges for interest rates. These ranges can be graphically characterized as "fans" or "bands" (ibid., pp. 415-416).

Sternlight (1994:116-117) also shows such ranges in similar graphical presentations, calling them "Levels and Targets (Cones and Tunnels)", and he also speaks about constructing a planned "reserve path" by assessing the reserve situation in the banking system during the day-to-day implementation of policy in the Fed.

Now, as Daane (1994:142-143) reveals, in the practical work of regulation the "ranges of growth of monetary and credit aggregates" that are nowadays set by the Federal Open Market Committee "for monetary policy" are quite wide. Accordingly, the process of trying to keep the values of M2, M3 and debt growth as well as - first and foremost - the interest rate within the target ranges often involve a fairly good degree of activism, discretionism on the part of the FOMC. Hence the small regulatory steps taken by the Fed indeed embody a good practical compromise between Keynesian discretionism and monetarist rulism. They apply activist, discretionist interference on a comparatively minor scale (relative to the size of the whole U. S. economy) in order to keep the variables within the target ranges composed with the help of certain rules. Although in the last analysis already leaning more towards Keynesian basic theoretical principles again, which is good news, the very functioning of the Fed today represents a kind of practical synthesis between Keynesian and monetarist ideas.

For that matter, however, as Hillier (1991:58) points out, Keynes himself "elaborated upon his views on how to control the economy in a series of articles for The Times in January 1937. ... His major proposal for stabilizing investment was to stabilize the long-term rate of interest, which 'must be kept continuously as near as possible to what we believe to be the long-term optimum'". This meant in effect a kind of rulism. However, as Hillier continues, "Keynes's other arguments in the articles for The Times indicated a degree of belief in activist policies entirely in keeping with the fine-tuning proclivities of later Keynesians". Hillier (ibid., p. 59) concludes that "although Keynes wished to develop institutional arrangements that increase long-term stability, he did not see these as substitutes for fine-tuning. He was quite prepared to propose a mixture of activist and non-activist policies at one and the same time. The Keynesians, therefore, in advocating fine-tuning policies were clearly taking their cue from their master." Thus Keynes himself developed a delicate synthesis between rulism and activism within his own system of ideas.

In a section with the title "Interest Rate versus Money Stock Targets" Hillier (1991:61) again points out that "Keynes proposed to use fiscal policy in a rather activist or fine-tuning manner, but ... he also, like many later Keynesians, favoured controlling the rate of interest in order to stabilize investment. Friedman, on the other hand, eschewed fine-tuning and proposed a simple policy of controlling the rate of growth of the money supply in order to stabilize the economy." As Hilier (ibid., p. 62) says, "it is not necessarily the case that aiming to fix the rate of growth of the money supply will stabilize the economy better than some other simple rule such as fixing the rate of interest."

Elsewhere Hillier (ibid., p. 193) quotes Buiter's (1980:47-48) opinion about the desirability of some measure of government activism: "There is no presumption at all that a government that sits on its hands and determines the behaviour of its instruments by the simplest possible fixed rules is guaranteed to bring about the best of all possible worlds". Even if rules are used from time to time, Hillier (1991:66) says, "which rule is to be preferred is partly an empirical issue and cannot be settled on purely theoretical grounds". Furthermore, "several proponents of intermediate targeting (of either the money supply, the interest rate or some other target) argue that targets should be set only over short periods, and that they should be adjusted frequently in the light of the changing behaviour of the economy" (ibid., p. 66). It seems that in the United States the Fed is currently regulating the economy in this way.

As regards the problem of rulism versus activism and the question of best targeting, it can also be interesting to look at what some representatives of the ascending trend of New Keynesian Macroeconomics say about it, in particular in connection with such a delicate topic as monetary policy. Mankiw (1994:1) writes that "(s)ome economists view monetary policy as a potential cure for economic fluctuations. Others would be satisfied if monetary policy could avoid being a cause of fluctuations." In the same volume Hall and Mankiw (1994) "discuss the role of rules in the making of monetary policy, especially rules aimed at targeting nominal income" (ibid., p. 1). As they say, "(t)here is increasing agreement among economists on two broad principles of monetary policy. The first principle is that monetary policy should aim to stabilize some nominal quantity. ... The second principle ... is the desirability of a credible commitment to a fixed rule for monetary policy ... rather than ... unconstrained discretion. ... One frequently advocated rule is targeting nominal income. Some ... advocate the complete suppression of discretion in monetary policy-making; others view the rules as more general guides and would give policymakers discretion to depart occasionally from targets." (ibid., p. 71). Hall and Mankiw (1994:91) conclude that "(a)lthough nominal income targeting is not a panacea, it is a reasonably good rule for the conduct of monetary policy".

It is interesting to observe how these New Keynesians aim at a compromise in the age-old debate between discretionism and rulism by promoting the use of nominal income as the main target of monetary policy. They thus suggest to make a most important ultimate goal of economic policy, the growth or high-level stabilization of nominal income, output, the rule itself to guide monetary policy targeting. It is also interesting that at the same time they claim the following: "the primary benefit of nominal income targeting is reduced volatility in the price level and the inflation rate" (ibid.). This looks like a promising compromise between Keynesian and monetarist goals in the widest sense, but with Keynesian primacy. It means that the targeting of a top Keynesian goal: stable high-level output, also satisfies - just as a by-product - a top monetarist goal: stable prices.

MONETARIST TENETS

The development of elements of some kind of a practical synthesis does not mean that a long and complicated theoretical controversy within the economics of the second half of the 20th century is over. Far from that. There is no possibility here, and it is not my intention, to take up or overview all issues along the vast frontline of debates between the opposing camps of the Keynesian and the monetarist traditions in economics. I only wish to tackle a handful of questions which I consider important.

Let us start with the argument that Krugman (1994:40) calls the monetarists' and specifically Milton Friedman's "effective line of attack on Keynesianism", "at the end of the 1960s". As Krugman ((ibid., pp. 40-47) writes, Friedman's (1968) successful theoretical attack refuted the widespread belief in the Phillips curve as a permanent, stable relationship, a trade-off between unemployment and inflation. The Phillips curve was a finding by A. W. Phillips (1958), but, according to Hillier (1991:150, 163n), "(t)he idea can be traced back earlier to Brown (1955) and Fisher (1926)"; the latter is also mentioned by Dornbusch and Fischer (1990:639n).

In even more comprehensive terms Friedman (1968:11) stated a "general conclusion" that the "monetary authority controls nominal quantities", among them "the quantity of money by one or another definition", and it can only "use this control to peg a nominal quantity"; but "it cannot use its control over nominal quantities to peg a real quantity", such as, among others, "the rate of unemployment, the level of real national income". As Krugman (1994:44) says, "Friedman was enunciating a familiar proposition, generally known as that of the neutrality of money. But ... he went on to turn it into a crucial policy idea".

According to Friedman's idea, expressed in a nutshell, a monetary expansion has real effects in increasing output only in the short run, because after a while all participants in the big game of market economy, both the firms and the workers, will raise the prices of their goods and services, selling prices and wage demands respectively, and then output will stop rising. The only final result is that the price-level has been raised. In this theoretical framework it is believed by economists that the "neutrality of money" phenomenon manifests itself in the long run, while in the short run a monetary expansion does have real effects in increasing output (as well), and not (only) prices.

As Krugman's (1994:43-47) witty analysis tells us, Friedman (1968) explains the difference with the thought that the participants of a market economy, "firms and workers" (Krugman 1994:44), are "fooled" by the first, demand-raising effects of a monetary expansion which "caught markets off guard" (ibid.). As Friedman (1968:10) himself puts it: "People have been expecting prices to be stable, and prices and wages have been set for some time in the future on that basis.". In other words, all participants of a market economy think for a while that it is only their own goods or services which are favoured by a sudden rise in demand, caused in fact by the generally increased money supply in the country. So they first only increase the volume of their products, goods or their hours of work performed, still at the old prices. Then it takes a longer time before the price level gradually rises in the whole economy, and as a result, real output stops increasing, and the "neutrality of money" phenomenon with stagnant output and only price-rises comes into prominence in the long run.

As Krugman (1994:43) points out, "Friedman took center stage by choosing to unveil his theory ... in a highly visible way, in his presidential address to the American Economic Association". But, as, for instance, Hillier (1991:152) mentions, similar ideas had already been published by Phelps (1967: cf. 254-257). Phelps (1968:678-683) continued to deal with this topic and he revealed that Friedman (1966:59) had even tackled the issue of "trade-off" earlier. The process Friedman and Phelps described led to a decisive theoretical victory by the monetarists from the late 1960s and even more from the early and mid 1970s onwards.

As Krugman (1994:45) sums it up: "Friedman argued that any attempt to use the Phillips curve to trade off higher inflation for lower unemployment would cause that curve to disappear: you would end up paying a higher and higher price in inflation for low unemployment, and when the price became unacceptable, you would discover that inflation would persist even in the face of high unemployment." Thus Friedman in fact predicted the possibility of the so-called stagflation phenomenon on the basis of people's gradual discovering and building in the higher prices in their inflationary expectations, and thus gradually moving away the 'unemployment for inflation' trade-off to new and new, more and more unfavourable, inflationary Phillips curves from time to time, in a few years' perspective. After the 1973 oil price shock due to the aftermath of the Yom Kippur war in the Middle East, the stagflation phenomenon indeed ensued in the economy of the United States.

As Krugman (1994:34-40) aptly analysed, the first great intellectual argument of monetarist attack on Keynesianism centred on the fact that "monetary policy works with 'long and variable lags'" (ibid., p. 36), and in consequence, discretionary government interference in the economy "does more harm than good" (ibid., p. 35). The second, "even more effective, line of attack"(ibid., p. 40) centred on the above-described process of gradual, adaptive price-rises after a monetary expansion, that is to say, the long-term, gradual restoration of the prevalence of the 'neutrality of money' principle. As a consequence, any discretionist monetary expansion with the aim of achieving full employment - as a trade-off along a Phillips curve - would time and again cause higher and higher rates of inflation.

As the essence of the first attack, one can say that instead of discretionary interferences, Friedman (1968:16) suggested his famous monetary rulism, the rule of "steady rate of monetary growth" (ibid.). As the essence of the second attack, one can say that instead of the possibility of aiming at lower unemployment via trade-offs between unemployment and inflation, Friedman (1968:8-9) introduced the notion of the "natural rate of unemployment" as a state of affairs to accept and preserve. Friedman introduced this notion on the basis of concocting a quite superficial analogy with and borrowing an attractive adjective from the Wicksellian idea of the "natural rate of interest". As Friedman (1968:8) says, "at any moment of time, there is some level of unemployment which has the property that it is consistent with equilibrium in the structure of real wage rates. At that level of unemployment, real wage rates are tending on the average to rise at a 'normal' secular rate , i.e., at a rate that can be indefinitely maintained so long as capital formation, technological improvements, etc., remain on their long-run trends. ... The 'natural rate of unemployment', in other words, is the level that would be ground out by the Walrasian system of general equilibrium equations, provided there is imbedded in them the actual structural characteristics of the labor and commodity markets, including market imperfections, stochastic variability in demands and supplies, ... and so on."

The essence of this definition is the supposition that "real wage rates are tending ... to rise ... at a rate that can be indefinitely maintained", which implies a constant rate of inflation. Apart from the difference of attributing a constant rate of inflation to the equilibrium state of affairs, that is to say, a stable rate of price-changes, instead of stable prices themselves, this definition is a rather orthodox statement reflecting a belief in the "Classical" or in another terminology "neoclassical" tenets of pre-Keynesian economics, a belief in the existence of an equilibrium at a constant rate of real wage inflation, despite "market imperfections". Any attempt to change the state of affairs at the "natural rate of unemployment" by external interference of "the monetary authority", can be successful only in the short run, but it is doomed to failure in the long run, according to Friedman (1968:9-11). In the long run the gradual, adaptive price-rises will reverse the initial increase in output and the initial decrease in the level of unemployment.

It is interesting to remark that the time perpective attributed by Friedman (1968:11) to the "temporary" or "initial effects" in the case of unemployment, if it is to be influenced by "a higher and unanticipated rate of inflation", is rather long and uncertain. We do not have any systematic evidence for that, he says, and as a "personal judgement", he assessed "the initial effects" to last "for something like two to five years"."This initial effect then begins to be reversed", he says, but the whole process of "full adjustment" takes "a couple of decades", at least "for changes ... of the order of magnitude that has been experienced in the United States" (ibid.).

As Krugman (1994:46) aptly characterized, instead of Friedman's "natural rate", "other economists, disliking the implied satisfaction with, say, 6 percent unemployment, have used such terms as the 'non-accelerating-inflation rate of unemployment', or NAIRU". Dornbusch and Fischer (1990:559n) mention this denotation as a "terrible terminology". It is "that unemployment rate at which inflation is neither accelerating nor decelerating" - they say (ibid.). This notion closely follows Friedman's (1968:8) definition, as "that level of unemployment" at which "real wage rates are tending ... to rise ... at a rate that can be indefinitely maintained".

Although Friedman's original definition did not put it explicitly, the process of gradual, adaptive price-rises he describes (ibid., pp. 9-11) implies an interplay between people's expectations about the price-level, that is to say, about the rate of inflation, and an unanticipated change in these parameters brought about by a sudden action of "the monetary authority". The full theory of the interplay between the expected and the experienced rates of inflation and its connection with the rate of unemployment was scrupulously worked out by Phelps (1967:254-257, 1968:678-683, 1971, reprinted in 1979b:97-107, and 1979a, reprinted in 1979b:93-95). These ideas are generally dealt with today under the name of "the natural rate hypothesis" (Phelps 1979b:101), going together with the hypothesis of adaptive expectations (Phelps 1968:682).

As a kind of summary of these ideas, one can read the lines written by Phelps (1979a:94): "The upshot of the natural rate hypothesis is that monetary and fiscal policies engineering faster growth of aggregate demand will make no permanent difference for the rate of unemployment: The equilibrium unemployment rate will not be permanently affected, and the actual unemployment rate will converge to its equilibrium path." As regards the "'adaptive' or 'error-correcting' theory of expectations", postulated by "Friedman and I", as Phelps (1968:682) puts it, he also briefly sums it up as "a dynamic mechanism by which the expected inflation rate adjusts gradually over time to the actual inflation rate" (Phelps 1967:254).

It is interesting to observe that by the early 1990s and in all likelihood even today, around the turn of the millenium, these ideas of the monetarist Friedman and Phelps seem to have been accepted and made part of what is usually called 'mainstream' economic theory, or rather doctrine, even followed by moderate Keynesian economists who are generally called New Keynesians today (cf., for instance, Hillier 1991:152-156; Dornbusch and Fischer 1990:480, 513-531, 558-559, 635-637; Heap 1992:46-54). Unfortunately, we can add, because steps taken towards a practical synthesis are one thing and surrender in theoretical questions is another.

NEW-OLD CLASSICALS

Friedman's and Phelps monetarist reasoning was developed further, to the extreme, by the rational expectations school and its intellectual leader, Robert E. Lucas, who can be regarded today as the main representative of contemporary conservative, "New Classical", macroeconomics. Instead of the adaptive expectations hypothesis of Friedman and Phelps, the New Classicals assert that, as Hillier (1991:157) sums it up, "agents do take into account readily available information such as government announcements of policies for that period, and make predictions about the effects of those policies; if those predictions are based on the correct model of the economy, then they are said to be rational expectations".

In his Nobel lecture, a characteristic brief summary of his ideas, Lucas (1995:1-5) starts by rightly pointing out that the difference or even contrast between the short-term and long-term effects of a monetary expansion, a situation of increased money supply, is a problem that has been keeping economists busy for centuries. He dates back the origins of the problem to David Hume's two essays in 1752 (reprinted in Hume 1970), and he points to the fact that while Hume clearly described the contrast between the long-term neutrality of money and its short-term real effects in increasing production, he did not attempt to analyse the causes and the process of formation of this difference in detail. As mentioned, Milton Friedman (1968) performed precisely such an analysis.

Lucas himself (1995:5-13 and 22-23) briefly traces the history of the question in 20th-century economics and sums up the conclusion of the rational expectations school, of which he can be considered the undisputed leader (for the main building stones in his oeuvre, see Lucas 1981). The summary of the rational expectationist standpoint is that not even the time dimension is relevant to making the difference between merely inflationary versus real, output-raising consequences of a monetary expansion. According to Lucas (1995:22), the outcome depends on the question whether the "changes in money growth" (ibid.) are anticipated or unanticipated. "Anticipated monetary expansions" have inflationary consequences, "but they are not associated with the kind of stimulus to employment and production that Hume described". "Unanticipated monetary expansions, on the other hand," - Lucas continues - "can stimulate production as, symmetrically, unanticipated contractions can induce depression" (ibid.).

According to the ideas of the rational expectations school, the reason is that in the case of anticipated changes all actors in the game of the market economy are well informed about the processes being under way and they all modify their expectations about the new price level very quickly. The long run in Friedman's (1968) chain of thought becomes very short run in this way, so there is no "initial effect" any longer, and in consequence there are no more real effects of a monetary expansion at all. So, the New Classicals not only retain monetarism, as Galbraith and Darity (1994:249) attribute it to them, but they are hyper or ultra-monetarists in the sense that they take the monetarist doctrines to the extreme.

According to them, there is no effect of any activist, discretionist interference at all, "as long as government policies are pre-announced or otherwise predictable", summarized in the words of Hillier (1991:159). "Only unpredictable events shock the economy away from the natural rate of unemployment" (ibid.). This tenet is generally called the "irrelevance hypothesis", meaning that government policies aimed at Keynesian aggregate demand management have mostly become irrelevant in our age, because "predictable government policy cannot affect real output and employment, but only nominal values" (ibid., p. 184).

Thus even today, as Hillier (1991:194) points out, "the debate still hinges upon the same issues as those at stake between Keynes and the Classics - the dynamic efficiency of the competitive market economy, and the potential role for government intervention". The apology of the former and the irrelevance of the latter are enshrined in the New Classical tenets of Lucas and his followers. This is the highly appreciated conservative political yield of the rational expectations school, the New Classical Macroeconomics, as this trend has become generally called (cf., for instance, Dornbusch and Fischer 1990:6, 29; Heap 1992:59-78). It is abbreviated as NCM by Heap (ibid.), who compares and analyses this trend paralleled with New Keynesian Macroeconomics, NKM.

As regards the general characteristics of the final conclusions of NCM, one can well turn to some works of its leading figure: Robert E. Lucas, Jr. One can find reasonings like this: "nonfrictional unemployment is ... 'voluntary'" (Lucas 1969, reprinted in Lucas 1981:42). In another article Lucas (1974, reprinted in Lucas 1981:156) asks: "Why is it that workers choose (under some conditions) to be unemployed rather than to take employment at lower wage rates?" His answer is: "... workers might rationally prefer some other activity to work at wage rates they perceive to be temporarily below normal". Lucas (1978, reprinted in Lucas 1981:245) repeats that "treating unemployment as a voluntary response to an unwelcome situation" is favourable, and instead of dealing with the problem of unemployment he pays tribute to focusing "discussion of monetary and fiscal policy on stabilization, on the pursuit of price stability ...". He concludes that "(t)he policy problem of reducing business cycle risk is ... one which I believe monetary and fiscal policies directed at price stability would go a long way toward achieving", while "(t)he pursuit of a full-employment target which no one can measure or even define conceptually cannot be expected to contribute to ...(a) solution ..." (ibid., p. 246).

It is perhaps in this article that Lucas expressed his view most pointedly that all unemployment must be voluntary and that "involuntary (or Keynesian) unemployment" simply does not exist. He bases his argument on questioning Keynes's original concept of involuntary unemployment, which was based on Keynes's assertion that "more labour would, as a rule, be forthcoming at the existing money wage if it were demanded" (Keynes 1936:7 and Lucas 1978, reprinted in Lucas 1981:242). At this point Lucas pretends not to understand what the term "the existing money wage" meant. He puts forward banal phrases like "we define an individual's wage rate as the price someone else is willing to pay him for his labor", in which case we must suppose that the worker does have a job, and is not unemployed, of course, just to make it possible for Lucas to measure his "existing money wage". Then, says Lucas, "Keynes' assertion above is defined to be false", that is to say, the worker's work was indeed in demand. What Lucas means here is that for a really unemployed worker there can be no such thing as "the existing money wage" because he is not in an employment situation that would actually measure it. If "existing money wage" can be perceived at all, there is no longer unemployment for the worker, he implies. Lucas simply pretends to have never heard about existing average money wage levels in various industries and occupations. In this key article about the allegedly meaningless quality of Keynes's notions of "involuntary unemployment" and about the uselessness of the generally used notion of "full employment" in an economy, Lucas seems to base his whole argument on a deliberate pretence of simple-minded thinking.

The arch-monetarist creed of Lucas (1995:23) manifests itself in his "much useful guidance", according to which, "(f)irst, pre-announced targets for the growth rate of monetary aggregates can be focused exclusively on inflation. (It goes without saying, of course, that such pre-announced targets can and ought to be attained.) Second, monetary policy that simply maintains a constant growth rate removes money as an independent source of real instability." For him it also goes without saying that "the main task of monetary and fiscal policy is to provide a stable, predictable environment for the private sector of the economy" (Lucas 1980, reprinted in Lucas 1981:260). On the other hand, he believes that "economic policy in the OECD countries in the coming ten years will involve a wide variety of government interventions", but the "chances that it will be economic theory which provides coherence to these policies must be judged ... to be near zero" (Lucas 1976, reprinted in Lucas 1981:269). Private sector good, government bad.

As Galbraith and Darity (1994:249) sum it up, "the new classical model combines three fundamental elements, or assumptions. Monetarism, the basic belief that the money stock is an exogenous policy variable and that money is neutral, is retained as the first of these. The other two are market clearing and rational expectations." The issue of monetarism is dealt with separately here, in another chapter.

As regards the perfect market clearing assumption, this means that NCM rejects "sticky wages, sticky prices, and lags in adjustment" (ibid.). NCM economists thus live in a last-century theoretical dream-world of Walrasian equilibria, where all markets clear simultaneously after the mediation of a great imaginary auctioneer. Such an economy only exists in fantasy. The busy occupation and the greatest success and merit of New Keynesian Macroeconomics, NKM, since about the 1980s have been the thorough refutation of the perfect market clearing assumption of NCM. Legions of evidence show the futility and erroneous character of this renewed classical dream (see, for instance, Mankiw and Romer 1991), and the NCM school may at long last have been put on the defensive in this question today.

As Howitt (1990:78) writes, "New Classical Economics did not succeed in providing a convincing explanation for why monetary policy should have more than fleeting real effects, or for why wages and prices should be so slow to respond to demand shocks". He also points out that "(t)he Lucas aggregate supply schedule that lies at the heart of New Classical Economics is now admitted by economists of all persuasions to be an empirical failure" (ibid., p. 79).

It has been comparatively easier to refute the perfect market clearing assumption of NCM than its tenet of rational expectations. The latter notion was coined by Muth (1961) but raised to the level of a major doctrine by Lucas (see, for instance, 1972). It assumes that all economic agents are highly rational, profit-maximizing, they always search, find and make use of all relevant information, and are always able to construct from them the best, perfect modelling of future economic events, on the basis of the only true economic theory, which is tacitly assumed to be NCM, of course.

The characteristic feature of NCM is that it vastly overestimates the possibilities of human knowledge and information about the economy. As Morgan (1978:3) points out, already Keynes "stressed in particular the role of uncertainty and expectations in ... an economy and the consequent information problems to which they gave rise". Morgan (ibid., p. 113) says that "(t)o Keynes the great problem facing rational men was uncertainty". He quotes Keynes (1937), who, among others, accused "the Classical economic theory" of trying "to deal with the present by abstracting from the fact that we know very little about the future" (ibid.). Among other traits, this characteristic feature also makes the New Classicals very similar to the old "Classicals" or "neoclassicals".

Indeed, both of these two different phrases are generally used to denote the same group of late 19th and early 20th-century economists. Keynes himself called the main trend of the generations of economists dominant both before him and at the time he started to work "classical economics". As Keynes (1936:3n) definitely explains: "'The classical economists' was a name invented by Marx to cover Ricardo and James Mill and their predecessors, that is to say for the founders of the theory which culminated in the Ricardian economics. I have become accustomed, perhaps perpetrating a solecism, to include in 'the classical school' the followers of Ricardo, those, that is to say, who adopted and perfected the theory of Ricardian economics, including (for example) J. S. Mill, Marshall, Edgeworth and Prof. Pigou.". Thus he included in this denotation both his predecessors and many of his contemporaries, and besides the names he mentioned their ranks also comprised, for instance, Walras, Pareto and Irving Fisher.

Another kind of terminology preserves the phrase "classical" for the great 18th and early 19th-century thinkers of economics: Adam Smith, the founder of the discipline of economics, David Ricardo, John Stuart Mill, and denotes the generation of Keynes's contemporaries, those dominant around the turn of the 19th and the 20th centuries, as "neo-classical" economists.

As Hillier (1991:193-194) writes, "the New Classical school may be characterized as assuming widespread economic knowledge on the part of both the government and private agents". However, as Hillier (ibid., p. 188) points out, the rational expectations hypothesis is in fact very implausible; "the man or woman in the street simply does not form rational expectations". Against this fact NCM usually replies with the argument that "for the theory to work, it requires only that a few important individuals, such as government officials, business and labour leaders, form rational expectations" (ibid.), however, in reality "there are several competing forecasting models with widely different properties" (ibid., pp. 188-189).

Hillier refers to B. M. Friedman (1979) (only the namesake of his well-known monetarist colleague), who points out that people's expectations are often formed through learning processes, but these usually produce adaptive rather than "rational" expectations. The same point is emphasized by Heap (1992:79, 100 and 152). Following the thoughts of B. M. Friedman, Hillier (1991:189) says that "(i)n the real world, circumstances, and policy stances, shift and change, and individuals have to form expectations with little evidence available to provide them with much confidence". Therefore "it is open to question whether expectations could ever be expected to converge on rational expectations" (ibid.). In fact "the real world is characterized by expectational confusion", we can rather conclude.

As Galbraith and Darity (1994:398-400) point out, in many economic events there are no objective central tendencies, averages at all in the sense that they are supposed to exist "independently of what" they are "expected to be" (ibid., p. 399). So, no 'rational expectations' can be formed about them because the subjective expectations of the participants themselves are very much part of the game. "They are creating reality, in the way that a herd of buffalo creates the reality of its own movement" (ibid., p. 400).

Keynes (1936:161) wrote that "(m)ost, probably, of our decisions to do something positive, the full consequences of which will be drawn out over many days to come, can only be taken as a result of animal spirits - of a spontaneous urge to action rather than inaction, ... ". The very characteristic phrase "animal spirits" has been picked up later by several authors, and they used it in various different but apposite senses. For instance, the passage about "animal spirits" also caught the attention of Scitovsky (1986:188) when he analysed people's economic motivations, just as Keynes had done. About the relationship of the topic of such motivations to the problem of uncertainty, see Matthews (1991) and Meeks (1991a) in particular. In connection with the question of the 'rational' character or not of people's expectations, according to Galbraith and Darity (1994:400), "economist Joan Robinson liked to say that the herd movements of investors and entrepreneurs can best be described as reflecting animal spirits".

Indeed, as Keynes (1936:148-163) wittily commented in detail on investment decisions, people's expectations are often rather volatile and subjective. As he puts it: "It is not a case of choosing those which, to the best of one's judgement, are really the prettiest, nor even those which average opinion genuinely thinks the prettiest. We have reached the third degree where we devote our intelligences to anticipating what average opinion expects the average opinion to be." (ibid., p. 156). This is indeed very characteristic even today. Precisely these words of Keynes are cited by Coy (1997:67) when he writes about the stock markets that "bubbles can form and burst because investors focus on one another instead of on the fundamentals". This is the true face of the expectations which are alleged to be "rational" by Lucas's NCM.

Howitt (1990:73) also points at this "component of Keynes's central message", namely, the "pervasive uncertainty" of investment demand. He, too, refers to the "'animal spirits' of entrepreneurs, which are subject to 'waves of optimistic and pessimistic sentiment'" (Keynes 1936:154, cited by Howitt 1990:73). Howitt adds: "The development of organized security markets exacerbates the instability of investment because 'certain classes of investment are governed by the average expectation of those who deal on the Stock Exchange, rather than by the genuine expectations of the professional entrepeneur', (p. 151) and those expectations are formed by forecasting the forecasts of others rather than being rooted in the fundamentals" (Keynes 1936:151 in Howitt 1990:73-74). Precisely because of this subjective character of expectations there are often no "fundamentals" at all, we can add.

Besides that, Howitt (ibid., p. 67) also points out that

"(p)hilosophers are raising important fundamental problems with the concept of rationality (e.g., Elster, 1979). Such problems become apparent in NCE when we ask what happens when an agent observes an event he had thought was impossible. The NCE methodology seems to deny the very possibility of such events." (NCE is New Classical Economics in Howitt's abbreviation, the same as NCM with Heap.)

To give a very brief, one-sentence, critique of the "rational expectations" assumption, one can say that it would only be - perhaps - valid if each and every participant in the market economy of a country were a Lucas-disciple economist.

As Krugman (1994:51) puts it: "Lucas's theory seems to fly in the face of our workaday perceptions about how firms and households really behave." Indeed, an excellent critique of the rational expectationist standpoint is given by Krugman (ibid., pp. 47-53 and 199-202). As Lucas himself (1995:23) admits, "there is an important ambiguity in...(the) conclusions, due to ambiguity in the term anticipated". We can add that this question depends on the information received or not received by the participants of the market economy. Krugman (1994:199-201) aptly points out that Lucas's handling of people's information is erroneous. Lucas, for instance, cannot explain at all the other side of the coin: why a cut in the money supply does produce a recession in real terms lasting for years, even though people get ample information about it. Such periods have been experienced in the real world. We can add that Lucas plays an arbitrary game with people's supposed information; he cannot give a satisfactory explanation why at one time information is supposedly quick and ample while at other times it is supposedly lacking or confusing. In Lucas's world people getting information or not always depends on the aim of the explanation.

When the question is why recessions in market economies of the real world are obviously not self-correcting according to the "classical argument" (Krugman 1994:47), Lucas says that people are "confused", which in fact means that they do not even notice an ongoing recession for years, and it thus remains "unanticipated" for years. But when it comes to discretionist government measures, they suddenly wake up, all become highly educated, shrewd Lucasian economists and instantly counteract the "anticipated" government actions by raising their prices and wage demands in a minute, in order to make a Keynesian cure futile.

Even though Krugman (ibid., p. 51) writes that "the rational expectations approach swept all before it, pushing Keynesians into an intellectual corner from which they have only recently started to emerge", he optimistically thinks that Lucas's dominance is over by now (ibid., pp. 201-202). But I believe that in practice the beneficial irrelevance of the "irrelevance hypothesis"-creating NCM is yet to come in the future. Unfortunately, Lucas's views are still often prevalent in both academic circles and the spheres of economic power in our Western world today, because the role of "political bias in making rational expectations macroeconomics attractive", that is to say, "its powerful conservative implications" (Krugman 1994:52-53) are overwhelming.

As Galbraith and Darity (1994:10) also say: "With the triple tools of monetarism, market clearing, and rational expectations, the new classical economists sought to demolish Keynesianism once and for all and to restore the basic noninterventionism policy conclusions that had prevailed among classical economists before the Great Depression. They almost succeeded. For fifteen years or so, until the late 1980s, the new classical economists dominated the theoretical side of macroeconomics, and they remain highly influential to this day."

Today employment can only be increased in their way, say the New Classicals, and many politicians, including leading right-wing Social Democrats, like Prime Minister Blair of the U.K. and Chancellor Schröder of Germany, still seem to fall for some of their tenets. The practical economic and political conclusions deduced from the doctrines of the NCM of Lucas and his followers are indeed forceful. They include deregulation of the labour market, decrease of wages and destruction of job safety as well as the fundamental weakening, breaking up or withering away of the trade unions. These trends want to put back the clock of history to about the early 19th century, the time of early capitalism, when individual labourers one by one faced the powerful, rich factory-owner and had to accept even the worst conditions of work to escape starvation. It is in fact a last-century image of the world, as a kind of example suggested for the present and for the future. A last-century future.

So, it seems to be in vain that scholars refute the new, fashionable dogmas of Lucas and the rational expectations school about the disappearance of the "short run", as, for instance, Krugman aptly does, because, unfortunately, in important places they are still the new, ruling orthodoxy today, in the late 1990s and early 2000s; in other words, these views are still widely shared in the main centres of economic and political power in the Western world. The possibility though cannot entirely be excluded that in some less powerful places these views are only announced and followed for reasons of "imitation to obtain legitimacy" (cf. Hedström 1998:309-312).

Or at least the New Classical dogmas seemed to be dominant up to about the autumn of 1998. Around this time appeared the first decisive signs of a breakthrough which is possibly making Krugman's optimism about an ongoing Keynesian reconquest come true. The signs of a possible change of times came after a Russian crisis, a World Bank report about Asia and an IMF prognosis about 1999. Since then, at long last, one could again read sound advice from time to time about lower interest rates, easier monetary policy and Keynesian measures even at the cost of budget deficits. No doubt the approaching threat of a looming world recession at that time forced that favourable change of mind.

KEYNESIAN DIFFERENCES

Before tackling the various shades of the Keynesian trend of economics, let me briefly recall the Swedish connections of Keynesian economics, without, however, classifying them by sub-trends of ideas.

As Weir and Skocpol (1985:130) point out, in Sweden "a key Social Democratic politician, Ernst Wigforss, along with some young Swedish economists, carried out policy-relevant deliberations on issues of unemployment in the later 1920s". This intellectual work engaged economists "including Dag Hammarskjöld, Alf Johansson, Gunnar Myrdal, and Bertil Ohlin ... " and these "younger economists ... would later come to be known as the 'Stockholm school'" (ibid.).

About the history of the new ideas at issue Weir and Skocpol (ibid., pp. 130-131) say: "The origins of breaks with orthodox neoclassical economics in Sweden have been the subject of vigorous debate among historians of economic thought. One position is that the Swedish economists arrived at new analytical understanding about possibilities for activist financial measures and the use of government deficits as a recovery tool by building on the indigenous Swedish theoretical tradition established by Knut Wicksell. ... An alternative interpretation is that Wigforss was inspired primarily by the English Liberals and Keynes and he in turn influenced the theorizing of the emerging economists of the Stockholm school. Whatever the precise lines of influence, however, it is obvious that,

....., important policy-relevant economic ideas were developed."

In their summary Weir and Skocpol (ibid., p. 132) say that this was the origin of and provided "the key to the Social Democrats' remarkable proto-Keynesian recovery strategy of 1933", and "it is difficult to imagine a better structural m trix for the crystallization of 'Keynesian' macroeconomic strategies several years before the appearance of The General Theory itself". Incidentally, according to a recommendation by Hillier (1991:72n), "(f)or a discussion of the relationship between the work of Keynes and the 'Stockholm school', see Patinkin (1982)".

My purpose in recalling these bright, progressive traditions in Swedish economics is to shed light on their sad contrast with our days, implied in the unfortunate fact that many or perhaps most Swedish economists around the turn of the millenium still subscribe to conservative, monetarist or New Classical doctrines.

That prominent Keynesian economist, the composer of the analytical model of "IS-LM" from Keynes's ideas, John Hicks, often refers to his Swedish connections. Howitt (1990:75) writes the following about the significance of IS-LM and Hicks: "The IS-LM apparatus that Hicks extracted from the General Theory has had an enormous effect on the development of macroeconomics. It is what distinguishes the economics of the past fifty years from what went before." According to Hillier (1991:42), "the terminology IS-LM was popularized by Hansen (1949), but the actual technique stems from an article published by Hicks (1937) a few months after the publication of the General Theory, of which it has now become the standard summary. Indeed, Keynes himself wrote to Hicks that he 'found it very interesting and really (had) next to nothing to say by way of criticism' (Moggridge, 1973, p. 79)".

When analysing Wicksell's monetary theory Hicks (1977:66) also speaks of "Wicksell's successors" and refers to the works of Lindahl and Myrdal. He calls Myrdal's "Monetary Equilibrium", "written and published in German" in 1933, and "appeared in English translation, in 1939", "the most important of post-Wicksellian writings" (ibid., p. 71). Hicks had already read the German version and even reviewed it (Hicks 1934, reprinted in Hicks 1982). As he writes in a prefatory note (Hicks 1982:42): "I was lucky that I had the Myrdal so early;

Keynes did not read it until the English translation appeared in 1939. It is clear, from some remarks recorded by Kahn ... that when he did read it he was quite impressed." About the relationship between the ideas of Wicksell and Keynes, Hicks (1977:72) reveals that "(a)s Keynes himself recognized, his model is nearer to Wicksell's than to any other with which he was familiar".

In an autobiographic writing Hicks (1979, reprinted in Hicks 1984) also reveals his readings of Swedish economics and his personal connections with Swedish economists. He says: "I managed enough German to read the Austrians, and also Wicksell and Myrdal (at that time only available to me in German). I have never learned Swedish, but, as will be seen, I have been deeply influenced by Swedish economics." (Hicks 1984:284). But, as he continues: "It was not only through books that one made these contacts. Eminent economists ... would come to the School (the London School of Economics). Thus it was that I made the acquaintance ... of Ohlin and Lindahl ..." (ibid.). Hicks also says about his own "dynamic model" that it "owes much ... to what I had got from the Swedes, from Myrdal and Lindahl". He explicates this theoretical help in detail and in a footnote says that "it was a great moment when I actually met him (Lindahl) at LSE. He had come to London to get help in the translation of his essays into English; I was able to find a helper for him." As he continues the story of the "helper", it turns out that "(a) year later, on another visit to see that helper, she had to tell him that we had decided to get married" (ibid., p. 286). The lady was obviously "Ursula Webb (Ursula Hicks after 1935)" (ibid., p. 282).

It is perhaps also worth mentioning that a prominent economist, Leijonhufvud (1967 and 1968), who, according to Hillier (1991:77), together with Clower "led an attempt to restore Keynes's status as an economist" after the so-called Neoclassical Synthesis, had to be in all likelihood of Swedish descent, judging by his surname (meaning 'lionhead' in Swedish). For that matter, this episode already leads us to the wider topic of the various branches of what can be called Keynesian economics, using this term now as an umbrella phrase.

As Morgan (1978:4) points out, "within a decade of the publication of The General Theory Keynesian economics had become the ruling paradigm", nevertheless a "divergence of views ... soon emerged between Keynes's analysis and that of his followers". As Galbraith and Darity (1994:8) say: "Despite the fact that the policies he advocated were widely implemented, Keynes's theoretical perspective was never embraced in full by the economics profession. In that sense, Keynes's revolution remains incomplete. The long history of 'Keynesian economics' has been one, in part, of repeated efforts to explain in simple, precise, and rigorous terms 'what Keynes meant', followed by repeated attacks both on these explanations and on the theoretical perspective behind them."

Morgan (1978:4) says that a "consensus of opinion ... gradually emerged in the debate between the supporters and critics of the Keynesian Revolution. This consensus involved compromising, to some extent, the revolutionary character of Keynesian economics and it has since become known as the 'neoclassical synthesis'. According to both Morgan (ibid.) and Hillier (1991:88), the main architect of this compromise was Patinkin (see 1956). As Hillier (ibid., pp. 87-88) says, "the model which Keynes presented in the General Theory was said to be a special case of the Classical theory in the presence of money-wage rigidities. This view minimized the importance of Keynes's theoretical contribution, but it was accepted that his contribution to the policy debate was important. ... Since such a view could be accepted by both Keynesians and those with Classical or neoclassical leanings, it came to be known as the Neoclassical Synthesis."

As Morgan (1978:4) asserts, "(i)n this synthesis some of Keynes's most important contributions are rejected, including, especially, his claim to have produced a more general theory than the classics". He says that in this framework "the two approaches are accepted as being essentially similar, differing only in the set of assumptions adopted". Namely, "it is claimed (that Keynes's assumptions) were ... more restrictive, i.e. less general, so the conclusion of the synthesis is that his analysis can be regarded as a special case of the more general classic theory" (ibid.).

"Keynes's analysis of uncertainty and expectations, and their relationship to and importance in a specifically monetary economy was overlooked and largely ignored" - Morgan (ibid., p.3) reveals. It is no wonder that "Keynesian economics soon succeeded in becoming the new orthodoxy" (ibid., p. 5) at that time.

Thus in the days before the "neoclassical resurgence" "in the late 1950s and 1960s", which "was basically anti-Keynesian" (Morgan 1978:5) and later developed into the victorious monetarist "counterrevolution" (a phrase of Galbraith and Darity 1994:9), the compromised 'Keynesian economics' in the form of the Neoclassical Synthesis had already become a lopsided, partial version of Keynesianism, a somewhat watered-down teaching, which omitted essential elements from the full spectrum of Keynes's original ideas.

For this reason the Neoclassical Synthesis was not the best kind of synthesis, despite the fact that it succeeded in becoming the mainstream economics, the dominant paradigm for several decades, and in spite of the usefulness of the analytical tools developed during this time. These latter included the simple "Keynesian cross" with the "consumption function" and the "multiplier", based on Keynes's notion of "the marginal propensity to consume", as well as the IS-LM model, composed from Keynes's ideas by "Sir John Hicks of Oxford" and named in this final form by "Alvin Hansen of Harvard" (Galbraith and Darity 1994:9).

Thus the Neoclassical Synthesis was a step or a half step backwards, to a somewhat more conservative type of economics. Keynes's full theoretical contribution was wider and more radical than that. According to both Hillier (1991:88, 100-114) and Morgan (1978:128-134), Clower (1965, 1969) and Leijonhufvud (1967, 1968) as well as Shackle (1967) had the lion's share in the efforts to restore the theoretical status of Keynes's original ideas. As Morgan (1978:112) says, "the task Keynes set himself was precisely that of rejecting Walras's law and the Walrasian system in general and of developing instead a monetary theory of output and employment in which uncertainty played a crucial role. Supporters of Keynes in this respect would include Robinson, Shackle, Davidson, Clower and Leijonhufvud ...".

According to Morgan (ibid.), "they can be contrasted with" the followers of what we call the Neoclassical Synthesis, which had become mainstream Keynesianism and the dominant economic paradigm for decades. Thus the original ideas of Keynes himself and of a few others mentioned can be contrasted "(w)ith those Keynesians such as Patinkin, Tobin, Samuelson, etc. whose refinements of macroeconomics have led to it becoming largely a highly specialised form of general-equilibrium theory ...". Morgan concludes: "Thus in the extreme we can view Keynes, Robinson, Shackle et al. the 'true' Keynesians ..." (ibid.)

Indeed, as Hillier (1991:108) also reveals, "the Neoclassical Synthesis offers an incorrect view of the General Theory. The General Theory did not simply propose a special case of the Classical model dependent upon rigid money wages. Rather, Keynes's was the more general model, since it did not assume stability about full employment, or instantaneous market clearing guaranteed by the presence of a Walrasian auctioneer. Instead, Keynes began to study the motion of the economy away from market clearing, without assuming that it would automatically move back to full-employment equilibrium."

Still, for some decades mainstream economics was dominated by "what Paul Samuelson called 'the neoclassical-Keynesian synthesis'", in the words of Sherman and Evans (1984:97), the followers of which "might be called neoclassical-Keynesians or, for short, neo-Keynesians". Sherman and Evans (ibid.) continue: "These neo-Keynesians are mostly in the United States, and most of them have tended to move back toward classical, right-wing laissez-faire policies. ..... Because they call themselves Keynesian, but are closer to the classicals in much of their analysis and policy recommendations, Joan Robinson calls them 'Bastard Keynesians'." In Sherman's and Evans's somewhat sharpened description the "split" of "the 'Keynesian' school into two warring factions" took place "(b)y the mid 1950s".

Joan Robinson (1973a:6) indeed criticized what she called "the vulgarised version of Keynes' theory" and spoke about "bastard Keynesians" (ibid.). She concludes her chapter in the starting 'stagflation' period and the ongoing ascension of monetarism to victory, in the early 1970s, with these bitter words: "Now, it seems that the bastard Keynesian era is coming to an end in general disillusionment; the economists have no more idea what to say than they had when the old equilibrium doctrine collapsed in the great slump. The Keynesian revolution still remains to be made both in teaching economic theory and in forming economic policy." (ibid., p. 11).

Today, as Mankiw and Romer (1991a:3) put it mildly, "the term 'Keynesian' can mean different things to different people". Indeed, with some degree of exaggeration one could say that as many kinds of Keynesianism exist as there are Keynesian economists, with a wide spectrum of theoretical, economic policy-making and general political views. James Tobin, for example, was allocated to the camp of the "dominant school" of "Keynesianism" or "modern Keynesians", together with Patinkin and Samuelson, as opposed to Keynes himself, by Morgan (1978:112); nevertheless, Professor Tobin is generally known as a scholar having some fairly brave, progressive views about economic policy and general politics at large, often expressed by him especially in the 1980s (see, for instance, Tobin 1987). As regards economic theory, "Tobin rejects rational expectations", according to Galbraith and Darity (1994:302n), and it is interesting to quote an opinion on another, in effect Post Keynesian, example of Tobin's progressive theoretical stance, by Sherman and Evans (1984:321): "James Tobin's tendency to identify money as a 'dependent' variable in his models classifies him as one who identifies the money supply as endogenous in both the short run and the long run" (cf. Tobin 1970 and 1981).

But in general terms it is by and large correct to distinguish broadly two main tendencies in the development of Keynesian ideas from the times after the publication of The General Theory in 1936 down to our days: a more compromising trend and a more radical trend. Particularly after the untimely death of Keynes in 1946 the compromising branch clearly got the upper hand. It became dominant in the form of the Neoclassical Synthesis, it became the mainstream of economics, the ruling orthodoxy, so to say, until about the late 1960s or rather the early or mid 1970s, when it was overthrown and replaced in this role by monetarism. The more radical versions of Keynesian economics have ever been in a minority, as regards both the number of followers and the general influence in theory and practice, down to our days.

As regards terminology, it is interesting to observe the evolution of the denotations of a few kinds of Keynesian economics. Sherman and Evans (1984:97) also reveal that opposed to what they abbreviate as "neo-Keynesians" after the full denotation of "the neoclassical-Keynesian synthesis", attributing the phrase to Samuelson, "(o)n the other side, there is the school called Post Keynesian". They immediately add: "This terminology is somewhat confusing because the Post Keynesians claim to be (and probably are) closer to the original writings of Keynes than are the neo-Keynesians." This remark is very apposite, indeed, the prefix "post" rather means that something is over, it has been transcended, put aside, even perhaps rejected; and at any rate, it rather means demarcation from the base-word or perhaps its negation than its continuation or renewal. This characteristic of the prefix "post" also gives ground to a possible etymological explanation of the term "Post Keynesians", because for several decades those economists calling themselves "Keynesians" were mainly the followers of the Neoclassical Synthesis (cf. Leijonhufvud 1967 and 1968), and it was possibly their views that the radicals wanted to transcend by using the prefix "post".

However, if one considers the original writings of Keynes himself as a starting point, then the terminology used in a key chapter with critical opinion on monetarism written by "the first American economist to be awarded the Nobel prize", as Gill (1976:141) put it, that is, by Paul A. Samuelson (1973a, reprinted in Gill 1976:143) is much better. There Samuelson writes that "my reading of the development of modern economic doctrine does not suggest to me that the post-Keynesian position that I myself hold, and of which Professor James Tobin of Yale and Franco Modigliani of M.I.T. are leading exponents, has been materially influenced by monetarism". Then in a passage with the title Post-Keynesianism and in subsequent passages Samuelson denotes the trend to which he also belongs as "the post-Keynesian economists", also adding with some self-irony: "which is to say ... the ruling orthodoxy of American establishment economics" (ibid., p. 146). In a few ironic words later in the text Samuelson (ibid., p. 149) also mentions, as a pure imaginary, theoretical pole, "an ultra-Keynesian model" as "the kind of Keynesian model that only a Radcliffe Committee member could still believe in".

This is in fact an unintentional reference to the minority radical trend of Keynesians.

From the view-point of pure grammar, namely semantics, Samuelson's (ibid., pp. 143, 146) denotation of his own trend as "post-Keynesian" was much better than the terminology that came into general usage in real life. Instead, real life went the other way round, in the way Sherman and Evans (1984:97) indicated: the followers of the more radical minority trend have been calling themselves Post Keynesian, while those who are in effect the theoretical successors of the "neoclassical-Keynesian synthesis", that is to say, the followers of the more moderate majority branch of Keynesianism, who have been on the way up from about the 1980s onwards, call themselves today New Keynesian.

The New Keynesians by and large follow in the footsteps of "the Keynesian consensus of the 1960s", as Mankiw and Romer (1991a:1) somewhat euphemistically call what was in fact the 'Neoclassical Synthesis', even though one page later these two prominent New Keynesians mildly ironize about their predecessors, saying that "most of the Keynesian economics of the 1970s imposed wage and price rigidities on otherwise Walrasian economies" (ibid., p. 2).

Galbraith and Darity (1994:10) briefly sum up the story of the recent development of mainstream economics, after the success and theoretical dominance of the new classicals in the late 1970s and in the 1980s, in these words: "... the initiative shifted with the emergence of yet another group in the late 1980s. This group, in conscious imitation of and opposition to the new classicals, has taken the designation of new Keynesians." We can add that, sadly enough, the "imitation of" and a degree of mesmerization by their opponents, the new classicals, is still somewhat wider than the mere issue of their name.

Unfortunately, the survival of the age-old controversy between different shades of Keynesianism may take on some traits of over-harsh criticism from time to time, and this does not help the development of Keynesian economics.

The New Keynesians, who are in the majority, sometimes belittle the Post Keynesians, as, for instance, the otherwise excellent Dornbusch and Fischer (1990:704) do in a tiny, merely half-page section devoted to them within a voluminous, great book: "Post-Keynesians are a diverse group of economists who share the belief that modern macroeconomics leaves aside or explicitly assumes away many of the most central elements of Keynes's General Theory. ... Post-Keynesian economics remains an eclectic collection of ideas, not a systematic challenge like, for example, the rational expectations equilibrium approach." The final words here are almost scolding, saying that "the deliberate down-playing, indeed rejection, of individual rationality and maximization as a basis of behavior by firms and households by post-Keynesians has kept the approach at odds with the mainstream of the profession, which has been attempting to bring macroeconomics into closer touch with microeconomics". In the later two editions of the book Dornbusch and Fischer (1994) as well as Dornbusch, Fischer and Startz (1998) do not devote a single passage to the Post Keynesians. (For that matter, they reduced their material generally in the later editions of the book, and this is why I mostly, though not exclusively, refer here to the 1990 edition; I regard this as the most complete version of their work.)

It is a little strange but obvious that some leading New Keynesians may feel much more respect towards their main contemporary antagonists: the rational expectationist New Classicals, than towards the minority Post Keynesians, who should in fact be regarded as their allies.

Howitt's (1990:76) opinion strengthens the impression that Post Keynesians are mostly stricken by belittlement: "The post-Keynesians ... are generally regarded by mainstream Keynesians as beyond the fringe." Fortunately, however, not all "mainstream Keynesians" share this view. Heap (1992:8), for instance, who is clearly New Keynesian, writes the following: "Economics is fractured into an orthodoxy and its critics; and the latter takes the former seriously in a manner which is rarely reciprocated. ... I have written this book within the orthodoxy, so to speak, because this has been the modus operandi of the NKM. However, ... there is little in the NKM which has not been well understood, albeit in a different and often less formal manner, in Post Keynesian circles for a very long time. ... I wish only to record the intellectual debt to Post Keynesianism now because it will go largely unacknowledged in the rest of the book."

Galbraith and Darity (1994:10) give a brief description of "another group of macroeconomists" as follows: "This group, usually known as post-Keynesian, is distinguished by its strong continuing interest in certain theoretical and policy issues that the other groups have tended to neglect. In particular, post-Keynesians predicate their analysis on a world of uncertainty, in which public policy plays a powerful function of coordinating and shaping the expectations ... Post-Keynesians believe that their formulations of macroeconomics are both closer to that of Keynes himself and more relevant to the politics of the modern world than are those of the other disputants. The post-Keynesian group is smaller and in many ways less influential than the Keynesians, monetarists, new classicals, and new Keynesians, but ... their views are important. The post-Keynesians reject rational expectations ... ". Later they also say: "Post-Keynesians claim to be the most direct descendants in the Keynesian tradition. They attack two pillars of the new classical temple: rational expectations and monetarism. The third pillar, market clearing, is considered a moot point. Unlike both the new Keynesian and the new classical schools, post-Keynesians do not believe in a single unified labor market. Some post-Keynesians believe that the money supply is endogenous and that monetary authorities are obliged to supply whatever quantity of money is demanded." (ibid., p. 440).

It is not my intention to tackle all the main ideas of the Post Keynesian trend here (for a good summary, see, for instance, Galbraith and Darity 1994:440-442). From the view-point of promoting reconciliation between various Keynesian schools and even the possible formation of common approaches, it is more interesting to know what the Post Keynesians, including Galbraith and Darity (1994:299 ff) themselves, say about the dominant New Keynesians. (Incidentally, as regards the surname Galbraith, I take the liberty to note that James K. Galbraith is the third good economist I have got to know with this name, the first being John Kenneth Galbraith, the well-known author of "The New Industrial State", criticized somewhat harshly by Krugman 1994:13-14, and the second John Alexander Galbraith in Canada.)

Reconciliation between the main Keynesian trends as well as the possible formation of common standpoints can perhaps be promoted by selecting progressive and realistic elements from both the New Keynesian and the Post Keynesian theoretical approaches, after constructive criticism.

According to Galbraith and Darity (1994:10), "(t)he new Keynesians accept many of the theoretical arguments of the new classicals...". Indeed, they accept too many of these, and this is their main weakness. Above all they can be accused of accepting two basic assumptions of the New Classicals, their supposed fierce contemporary antagonists, namely "monetarism" and "rational expectations". The New Keynesians only disagree with the New Classicals about the third "pillar" of "the new classical temple", to use the words of Galbraith and Darity (1994:440), the issue of market clearing. The NCM assumes perfect market clearing, while the New Keynesians emphasize the imperfect character of markets, with rigid, sticky wages and prices. It is in consequence of this that they "reject the idea that markets self-adjust to ensure full employment", as Galbraith and Darity (1994:10) put it.

As regards the rigidity of the most important market, the labour market, Galbraith and Darity (1994:304 ff) quote and explicate in detail Robert Solow's (1980) "December 1979 presidential address before the American Economic Association" which, as they assert, "crystallized the new Keynesian position". The later Nobel laureate Solow gave six multifarious reasons "for the stickiness of wages", these covering the cases of both real wages and money wages and various causes originating in characteristic behaviour types on either the workers' side or the employers' side or both. There is no doubt that here the New Keynesian argument is absolutely superior to the New Classical one, both theoretically and empirically, and as Hillier (1991:192) sums it up: "a sluggish adjustment of money wages and prices can cause the economy to diverge from full employment for lengthy periods of time". No doubt that "(i)n such cases fiscal and monetary policy changes, anticipated or not, can have real effects on the economy by affecting the level of aggregate demand" (ibid.).

However, the problem is that still around the turn of the millenium some even nominally Social Democratic governments in Europe follow defeatist strategies covered by misleading slogans like "new labour" (first and foremost the Blair government in the U. K. and the Schröder government in Germany) and are reluctant to pursue Keynesian aggregate demand management policies to cure unemployment. Instead, they fall for and follow New Classical arguments and try to decrease unemployment by applying measures of labour market deregulation, "liberalization", "flexibility". All this follows the example of the United States, and parallel with and sometimes behind such government policies there is also a theoretical softening of the New Keynesian position.

Indeed, it is often considerably easier, cheaper and even quicker for a government to resort to labour market deregulation instead of bothering with complicated Keynesian aggregate demand management policies. This is why contemporary governments often prefer to follow the advice of New Classical experts, and even New Keynesian experts flirt with the temptation of approaching the NCM position. If a rigid labour market is the only or the main reason for unemployment, then why not listen to the New Classicals and deregulate, since this often seems much easier than increasing aggregate demand á la Keynes. Even more so, if one in addition gives in to the NCM's monetarism and believes that after a while unemployment will return to the "natural rate" anyway.

However, the consequence of such theoretical surrender and the resulting defeatist governmental economic policy is misery for a great many people. The consequence is that in such countries, as Esping-Andersen (1996:2) writes, a "trade-off does exist between egalitarianism and employment". Later he explicates: "Europe's single largest problem is chronically high unemployment, while in North America it is rising inequality and poverty. Both symptomize what many believe is a basic trade-off between employment growth and generous egalitarian social protection. Heavy social contributions and taxes, high and rigid wages, and extensive job rights make the hiring of additional workers prohibitively costly and the labour market too inflexible." (ibid., p. 3). Still later he adds some more details: "The combination of high wage costs (due to mandatory social contributions) and rigidities (such as job tenure, costly termination payments, or generous social benefits) is widely regarded as a main impediment to job growth." (ibid., p. 8).

In a subsequent work Esping-Andersen (1999:122) reveals that "the package of (labour market) regulations can be regarded as the labour market equivalent to social citizenship rights", but "(t)he neo-liberal position is that labour markets, as a result, have become too rigid and that this is especially harmful in times that call for maximum and swift adaptation". As he says, "(t)o most contemporary economists, the crux of our employment problem is that labour markets are too inflexible" (ibid., p. 123). These "contemporary economists" mostly follow the New Classical school, we can add, but what is disquieting is the fact that the New Keynesians, having thoroughly analysed and proved the existence of wage (and price) rigidities, as mentioned above, sometimes (or perhaps still too often) fail to distance themselves from the politically conservative New Classical conclusions suggesting deregulation in the labour market as the main solution. In order to develop a progressive, synthetized, modern Keynesian standpoint, the New Keynesians should put more emphasis on activist demand management policies to be pursued by governments to cure unemployment sustained by imperfect markets, that is to say, wage and price rigidities.

The temptation for some New Keynesians to accept policy recommendations of labour market deregulation as a remedy for unemployment is so much the greater if, as may be concluded from the analysis of Galbraith and Darity (1994:299, 302, 389, 392), they are inclined to accept two basic assumptions within the theoretical arsenal of their supposed antagonists, the New Classicals, namely "monetarism" and "rational expectations". Then, following some erroneous conclusions of the NCM arguments, the only main cause of unemployment is believed to lie hidden in wage rigidities, and the ideological pressure for labour market deregulation, "liberalization", may become very strong indeed. (For a profound criticism, on empirical grounds, of the deregulation or "structural" concept see, for instance, Johansson et al. 1999b:31-73, 84-88, in particular).

"Monetarism" in this respect mainly involves Friedman's (1968) ideas about the long-run neutrality of money, and also Phelps's (1967 and 1968) similar thoughts about the refutation of a long-term possibility of a trade-off between unemployment and inflation on the basis of the Phillips curve, as well as the "natural rate of unemployment" hypothesis built on these tenets. Unfortunately, these doctrines are generally accepted today even in New Keynesian circles as valid descriptions of the long-term situations and processes in a market economy. This means that monetary expansions are generally supposed to work only in the short run.

Earlier in this work the usefulness of elements of a practical synthesis between Keynesian and monetarist views of monetary policy was mentioned. In contrast, it has to be emphasized now that not all kinds of syntheses are useful. A drift towards a bad, defeatist theoretical "synthesis" can also be imagined, in which NKM surrenders to some basic elements of NCM: "monetarism" and "rational expectations", without putting up a theoretical fight.

Instead of giving in to the new Classicals on at least two main points, the progressive way of development for the New Keynesians would be a good synthesis with the Post Keynesian Macroeconomics (PKM). The name of a united trend could be, for instance, "Modern Keynesians", in order to depart from the imitation and the spell of the "New" Classicals and also to get rid of the ambiguous prefix "Post". Or, in another solution, Post Keynesians could simply merge into the majority New Keynesian scientific circle if the latter agreed to modify their stance on some essential points.

Such a useful synthesis could involve by and large the following main points of a theoretical program for the New Keynesians as well as the Post Keynesians:

1./ Do not draw NCM type of conclusions about "deregulation" from wage rigidities. Draw Keynesian conclusions of aggregate demand management.

2./ Reject the many times refuted tenet of "rational expectations". Accept the realistic role of subjective expectations, often nicknamed today "animal spirits", and once thoroughly analysed by Keynes.

3./ Reject "monetarism" which mainly involves the acceptance of Friedman's and Phelps's "natural rate of unemployment" hypothesis, even in the milder, "long-run", monetarist version, let alone the "short-run", NCM version with the "irrelevance hypothesis".

4./ Accept the most essential contribution of PKM to economic theory: serious suggestions about the frequently endogenous characteristics of the money supply.

5./ The Post Keynesians should accept the New Keynesian emphasis on the importance of refuting false beliefs in perfect market clearing and they should give up any objection to the concept of a single unified labour market. Centralized wage-talks covering a unified labour market can and should be an important part of incomes policies and general incomes agreements to prevent leapfrogging wage-cost-push inflation.

The second point will now be tackled in this section, while the "long-run", monetarist version of the "natural rate of unemployment" hypothesis will be dealt with in the next chapter and the topic of endogenous money supply in a later chapter.

According to Hillier (1991:178), the 'New Keynesian' models "accept the rational expectations idea". Elsewhere he repeats that "New Keynesian models are those which accept the hypothesis that expectations are formed rationally, but reject the market-clearing assumption of the New Classical school" (ibid., p. 190). Only later does he slightly alleviate the statement by saying: "It is interesting to note that most of these New Keynesian models adopt the assumption of rational expectations, which provides a useful illustration of how the different schools respond to one another." (ibid., p. 195). While the interplay between NCM and NKM is also noticed and is a basic theme in the work of Heap (1992), the latter excerpt of Hillier's (1991:195) at least suggests that not all New Keynesians accept or adopt the most typical NCM assumption of "rational expectations". There are exceptions and indeed this is the heartening picture one can get from studying the selected writings of some authors of the NKM trend.

In the "Series Foreword" to Mankiw's and Romer's (1991b, 1991c) edited volumes, Benjamin M. Friedman and Lawrence H. Summers speak about "'nonrational' expectations" and "expectations based on less than full and symmetric information" as features incorporated in the analyses within the volumes. In one of the studies Cooper and John (1988, reprinted in Mankiw and Romer 1991c:3) assert in a short classification that "articles in the Keynesian tradition suggest that unemployment arises from nonrational expectations or wage and price rigidities". It is interesting to read Bryant's (1983, reprinted in Mankiw and Romer 1991c:25) prefatory note to his work, which has a mixture of "rational-expectations" and Keynesian characteristics: "Our Keynes-type model has two crucial ingredients, specialization and imperfect information." "Imperfect information" is also the key assumption in the work of Stiglitz and Weiss (1981, reprinted in Mankiw and Romer 1991c:247-276). N. Gregory Mankiw, a leading scholar of the NKM trend, speaks of "the importance of assymetric information for credit markets" (Mankiw 1986, reprinted in Mankiw and Romer 1991c:277).

The existence or even predominance of "nonrational", imperfect and assymetric kinds of informations in various spheres of the economy implicitly refutes the "rational expectations" assumption of NCM, because the universal availability of instant and perfect information is presumed to be a precondition of the rule of "rational expectations" in the economy within the doctrines of NCM. We can conclude that, fortunately, not all New Keynesians subscribe to "rational expectations" under the influence of NCM, but it would be desirable that the number of those New Keynesians who still do gradually diminished to zero.

NO "NATURAL RATE"

The theoretical standing of New Keynesian Macroeconomics, NKM, in opposition to the New Classicals will remain rather feeble as long as the Friedman-Phelps hypothesis of the "natural rate of unemployment" belongs to NKM's store of generally accepted theoretical tenets. The natural rate hypothesis has some fundamental flaws.

At any moment of time there may be a discrepancy between full employment (or rather almost full employment, with the deduction of transitional, "frictional" joblessness from the "full employment" labour force) and the level of employment corresponding to the so-called "natural rate" of unemployment. It is right to speak of "frictional unemployment" or "structural unemployment" (cf. Dornbusch and Fischer 1990:475, 552-553), but it is erroneous to make it identical with Friedman's and Phelp's "natural rate". The sheer numbers belonging to the "natural rate", for instance, up to 6, 8 or 10 percent or even higher unemployment in developed Western countries allegedly being "natural", should raise some suspicion. Another strange factor is that in figures explaining the "natural rate", the theoretical processes depicted as taking place whenever governments try to use aggregate demand management, always start, so to say, on the 'wrong side' of the vertical line of the "natural rate", allegedly identical with the full employment level of output.

Such figures usually have total output on the horizontal axis and inflation on the vertical axis, with downward sloping aggregate demand curves and upward sloping aggregate supply curves. The latter are usually based on Phillips curves augmented with adaptive expectations about inflation. Each curve corresponds to a certain level of expected inflation. Sometimes such a figure shows the Phillips curves themselves, and in this case the whole figure is mirrored around a vertical axis, compared to the normal output-inflation figure mentioned. In other words, plotting the Phillips curves, the higher level of unemployment is to the right and the higher level of employment to the left; while in the normal output-inflation figures both employment and output grow to the right along the horizontal axis, of course. Inflation is on the vertical axis in both cases.

Now, one can observe that supposed government actions in the theoretical explanatory figures always start on the higher employment side compared to the vertical line of the "natural rate", that is to say, in figures with Phillips curves to the left from the vertical line, and in the output-inflation figures to the right from the vertical line (cf., for instance, Hillier 1991:152-154; Dornbusch and Fischer 1990:524-534, 633-637). Then usually some diminishing spiral-shaped curves go around in these theoretical explanatory figures and show the full courses of the Friedman-Phelps long-run processes of "adjustment". While the starting point is always at a higher level of employment, that is, a higher output level, (or sometimes on the vertical line), the end-point is always on the vertical line, on the "natural rate" of unemployment, that is, the alleged "full employment" and therefore logically "full output" level (cf., for instance, Hillier 1991:153; Dornbusch and Fischer 1990:529, 534, 634, 636).

For the monetarists the purpose is to show that at the end of the full process of "adjustment", the level of employment, that is, output, has not increased, but rather decreased, and the only final result is that inflation has increased. So, the endpoints of the full courses of the Friedman-Phelps "adjustment" processes should always be on the vertical line of the "natural rate", but at a higher inflation level. Behold! How futile it is to try to increase the level of employment and output by aggregate demand management, be it a monetary or a fiscal expansion. Such government actions make no sense at all. The long-run result is only the "natural rate" and higher inflation. And NCM even says that such is the result already in the short run, so any anticipated government action is completely irrelevant. As regards NKM, unfortunately it seems to give in at least to the classical monetarist argument, which means long-term irrelevance with the possibility of short-term activism.

As was said earlier, the starting points are either on the vertical line or on the higher employment side compared to it, and the processes start in the direction of increasing employment and output. But are these governments really crazy? Do they obstinately try to increase full employment, that is, an already maximal output even further and further? According to the explanations they evidently try that; they act on the 'wrong side' compared to the vertical line of "full employment", that is, logically, the supposedly maximum output level. Do they want to cause overheating at any cost? The Friedman-Phelps "natural rate" hypothesis makes us believe so. It is unfortunate that this erroneous theory has obviously found its way into the very heart of NKM, into the store of its accepted main tenets.

Some suspicion is perhaps not unfounded that there is a hidden, ultimate, at least subconsciously ideological purpose behind the whole "natural rate of unemployment" hypothesis: to be able to claim that even comparatively high unemployment levels can be "natural". Thus, it is claimed, nothing can be and nothing should be done about such high unemployment levels. Only inflation should be fought, being the main or the only problem. This is the rich man's economics.

In reality the activist governments are not crazy at all. Although it is not easy to determine what should be considered full employment in any country at a certain time, it is wrong in principle to accept Friedman's and Phelps's "natural rate of unemployment" as the full employment level, or even the 'almost full' employment level, that is to say, the "frictional" or "structural" unemployment level (cf. Dornbusch and Fischer 1990:552).

Friedman's copying of Wicksell's "natural" adjective was not a good idea. It is better to use the more modest though somewhat odd expression abbreviated as NAIRU. (For a thorough empirical criticism of the "NAWRU" measure, which is very similar to "NAIRU", see Johansson et al. 1999b:31-73.) Or it is even better to speak about "the steady-state equilibrium level" which "the unemployment ratio" "must approach", according to Phelps (1967:256). There may be times in the economy of a country when the inflation rate happens not to be accelerating (or decelerating) but to be more or less constant for a period. But it is not at all certain and nothing on earth guarantees that such a "steady state" always happens to be at the point of maximum output, that is to say, at full (or in practice almost full) employment level, in other words, at "frictional" or "structural" unemployment level. Such a "steady state" of inflation may occur at any level of output, employment and unemployment.

Think of it: according to the underlying adaptive expectations hypothesis of Friedman and Phelps, the only precondition of such a "steady state" is that people's inflationary expectations happen to be the same as the actual rate of inflation. This is a definition which is quite independent in principle of any state of full employment or not, and even of any actual size of unemployment. Suppose that people's inflationary expectations happen to be exactly fulfilled for a while at an unemployment rate of 20 percent or 30 percent. Is that the "natural rate of unemployment" then?

The "natural rate of unemployment" hypothesis in fact rests on some rather vague psychological foundations. People's expectations about any kinds of economic factors are rather volatile, they can easily be influenced by any events, by anything. For an expert opinion on this question see, for instance, Keynes's (1936:148-158) about the frailty and ridiculousness of people's expectations in connection with investment markets.

There can indeed be times when people's subjective expectations about the rate of inflation happen to coincide with the actual rate of inflation, and no adaptive, extra price-rises of the kind Friedman (1968:10) described are taking place. The level of output and employment may then also stay at a "steady-state" point for a while, but nothing guarantees that this is a full-employment equilibrium. Such points may have considerably greater rates of unemployment than the "frictional" or "structural" level supposed to belong to full employment. As Morgan (1978:133), analysing Keynes's original ideas, puts it: "the system does not return to general equilibrium because there will still exist an excess supply of labour - Keynes's 'unemployment equilibrium'". Then he adds in a note: "Involuntary unemployment obviously implies that the labour market is not in equilibrium so that here 'equilibrium' should be taken to imply 'no tendency to change'. Keynes was not therefore talking about a static equilibrium in the sense that all markets are cleared but rather the tendency of some markets to remain persistently in disequilibrium." (ibid., p. 170).

Keynes (1936:249-250) himself characterized such a state of affairs as follows: "... it is an outstanding characteristic of the economic system in which we live that, whilst it is subject to severe fluctuations in respect of output and employment, it is not violently unstable. Indeed it seems capable of remaining in a chronic condition of sub-normal activity for a considerable period without any marked tendency either towards recovery or towards complete collapse. Moreover, the evidence indicates that full, or even approximately full, employment is of rare and short-lived occurrence."

Thus governments are entirely justified if they want to move the economy out from such a "chronic condition", by discretionary actions, either monetary or fiscal expansions, by increasing output via aggregate demand management, in order to approach a genuine full employment situation, that is, to diminish unemployment to its 'frictional' or 'structural' level. They are not foolish for not accepting and trying to disturb the prevalence of a supposed "natural rate of unemployment", to which the economy would allegedly return anyway. It is not overheating that they want to generate, because the alleged "natural rate" is not full employment at all, it is only a more or less "chronic condition of sub-normal activity".

As Howitt (1990:72) briefly puts it: "The system is not, to use a phrase that Keynes liked, self-adjusting. Instead, government intervention is needed to eliminate involuntary unemployment." Then Howitt continues: "Keynes tried to support this claim with the idea of quantity adjustment as an equilibrating process. Following a disturbance to aggregate demand the ensuing quantity adjustments will not continue forever until a position of full employment or complete collapse is reached, but will generally lead to an equilibrium at less than full employment." (ibid.).

Friedman (1968:8) might have in secret felt such a possibility in his guts, because he in effect put a qualification into his definition of the "natural rate of unemployment" when he said: "including market imperfections". However, he still went ahead with the fabrication of his imperfect notion and denoted it with the tempting adjective "natural", which he had obviously fallen in love with, having borrowed it from Wicksell. In reality Friedman's and Phelps's "natural rate" hypothesis only describes points of "no tendency to change", in other words, points of 'Marshallian equilibrium', when not all markets clear, as opposed to the imaginary Walrasian equilibrium, when all markets are dreamed to clear. And the most important market, the labour market, can obviously be far from clearing at such points; there can be unemployment of considerable size there, and this is far from being "natural". Such a state of affars, even though it can continue "for a considerable period" in the words of Keynes, is not "natural" at all.

But what about the adaptive mechanism of gradual price-rises and their time-lagged effect of slowing down and later even reversing the initial increase in output after a governmental action to remedy unemployment by discretionist aggregate demand management, whether by monetary or fiscal means, of which the version of monetary expansion was so successfully analysed by Friedman (1968:10)? As Dornbusch and Fischer (1990:480-481) point out, there was a computer-experiment with a "macroeconometric model" of the U.S. economy in 1987. The results showed that "in the short run an increase in the money stock affects primarily output and has little effect on inflation or prices or wages", while "over longer periods of years, the impact of an increase in money is almost entirely reflected in prices and wages and very little in output" (ibid., p. 480). These results illustrate that Friedman's (1968:10) similar description certainly revealed an existing characteristic of monetary expansions, namely, the difference between the initial and the long-term effects, but this had already been revealed by Hume's two essays in 1752 (reprinted in Hume 1970, quoted by Lucas 1995:1-5, 26).

However, as the above-cited computer-experiment showed, the time-schedule of the reversing changes in output is rather long. Following the impact of a 0.5 percent monetary expansion "in the experiment, even after ... 4 years, output is still above its initial level" by about 1 percent, and "prices have not yet risen by a full percentage point" (Dornbusch and Fischer 1990:481). Judging from the figure there (ibid., Figure 13-7), after four years the process of "adjustment" still seems to be at around the first quarter of a supposed spiral (cf. ibid., pp. 529, 634, 636). Friedman (1968:11) himself assesses that "a full adjustment ... takes about ..., say, a couple of decades". Such a time perspective is uncontrollably long.

Suppose that output before a monetary expansion happened to be at the level corresponding to the "natural rate of unemployment" (cf. Dornbusch and Fischer 1990:636). Following a monetary expansion it is rather unlikely that after a couple of decades the end-point of the whole process of an "adjustment" will be at the same output level as it had been before the monetary expansion began; that is to say, the starting and ending points are strictly above each other on a vertical line showing output corresponding to a "natural rate of unemployment". To suppose that output is unchanged after a couple of decades is very strange indeed if one simply takes into account the general phenomenon of growth in modern economies (cf., for instance, Dornbusch, Fischer and Startz 1998:40-77). A few decades of complete stagnation in a modern country is a very unlikely supposition.

To put it another way: to get the end-points after such a long "adjustment" process exactly above the same levels of unemployment, employment and output again as the starting levels, one would need to suppose years of growth followed by or mixed with several years of recession. Even so there would only be a very little chance of seeing the same constellation as the initial one, and only if the observer waited patiently to be able to catch a moment when unemployment, employment and output happen to have the same levels as the initial ones, in order to declare an endpoint, whatever the shape of changes might have been in the meantime. And even this could happen only if many characteristics of the economy either remained unchanged or returned to the same state to make the connections between output, employment and unemployment precisely the same as at the starting point.

The precondition of the level of unemployment settling just at the "natural rate" is said to be that the actual inflation rate happens to equal people's expectations about it. Therefore the levels of employment and output corresponding to the "natural rate", allegedly full employment and logically maximum output, or as it is often called today, "potential output" (cf., for instance, Dornbusch, Fischer and Startz 1998:13-14), also have to depend on this precondition. And this can be satisfied only by chance.

There is a naive presupposition about the level of inflation, implied in the "natural rate" hypothesis. The underlying inflation level is tacitly supposed to be fundamentally stable, permanent if left alone, that is, without a monetary expansion, during the whole time period of "adjustment", which, as Friedman (1968:11) told us, may take a couple of decades. Inflation is tacitly supposed to depend on nothing else on earth than the adaptive price-rises of the adjustment process described by Friedman and Phelps, ensuing after a monetary expansion. And people's expectations about inflation are also supposed to depend on nothing else than this gradual process of adjustment. This is also a naive belief. The underlying or "background" level of inflation, that is, the level which is independent of a Friedman-Phelps adjustment process under discussion, is far from being permanent for a couple of decades. In real life it may well change from month to month. The same is true about people's expectations about the inflation rate; it can also change frequently, quite apart from any adjustment process at issue. And to top it all: nothing guarantees that the actual inflation rate and people's expectations about it will change together, in a congruent way, from month to month.

During a couple of decades a great deal may happen to the economy of a country. During such a long time both people's expectations about the level of inflation and the actual rate of inflation may change a few dozen times. Even if the supposition of adaptive expectations about inflation, which Friedman's and Phelps's doctrine implies, may from time to time be correct, this by no means ensures that expectations and actual inflation rate change together over long time periods. There is no guarantee that if and when they possibly and coincidentally become equal again, then both employment and output happen to be of the same level as they had been before an initial expansionary action started a few decades earlier. In addition, there may well be many different expectations about inflation at any time among both the experts and the people at large in every country. Expectations are rarely homogenous.

The monetarist idea of the natural rate of unemployment is also involved when, after the gradual, adaptive price-rises described by Friedman (1968:10) as taking place after a monetary expansion, there comes the phase of deliberate wage-rises negotiated, for example, by trade unions in answer to the perceived price-rises. Such processes can well be analysed using more conventional, "static", prices-output figures (when simply prices are on the vertical axis and not their speed of change, inflation, as in the Phillips curves). See, for instance, Hillier (1991:148, Figure 6.3) about a so-called cost-price inflationary spiral (only an abstract "spiral", not one seen in the figure) consisting of alternating cost-push and demand-pull phases, generated by rising wage costs and rises of aggregate demand via accomodating monetary expansions respectively. These are well-known processes in reality, but a frequent misbelief in connection with them bears the hallmark of monetarist influence with the "natural rate" hypothesis. It is the misbelief that after the alternating rounds of wage-rises and price-rises along series of aggregate demand and aggregate supply curves, the crossing points move upwards in the long run vertically above a point corresponding to one and the same permanent level of unemployment, that is, also of employment. Thus it is a misbelief that the crossing points mark the same permanent level of output all the time.

This is not necessarily the case at all. During the various rounds of wage-cost-push and demand-pull price-rises, unemployment, employment and output may change quite multifariously. In reality there is no "natural rate", no compulsory vertical line whatsoever around which the alternating rises and falls of output allegedly converge in the long run.

As regards empirical data, if one returns to the Phillips curves, that is, putting inflation on the vertical axis with unemployment on the horizontal one, and examines, for instance, the plotting of those data taken retrospectively from the development of the U.S. economy between 1961 and 1988, presented by Dornbusch and Fischer (1990:479, Figure 13-6), the zigzag shape of the curves shows that Friedman's and Phelps's prediction about the changing Phillips curves certainly came true; however, there is no trace of any kind of long-run convergence towards any kind of "natural rate of unemployment".

The late Arthur M. Okun (1991:340-343) called Friedman's and Phelps's above-described ideas "accelerationism". He reveals in a note (ibid., p. 372, note 12) that "the essential elements of the theory were spelled out much earlier" by Fellner (1959). As Okun (ibid., p. 340) says, it is "hypothesized that inflation will become increasingly rapid in any maintained situation in which unemployment lies below some critical, or 'natural', rate". In his summary of the argument he describes the belief that "the very possibility of getting unemployment under the natural rate depends on a process of fooling people ... (t)hrough lags in the perception of inflation, (the) surprises raise output and employment, but as people learn that they are being fooled, the lags shorten". As Okun admits, in the 1970s "(c)learly, the short-term Phillips curve has shifted upwards. In the sense of recognizing that shift, we are all accelerationists now (to reverse Friedman's celebrated concession to Keynes)." (ibid.).

But Okun (ibid., p. 341) points out that the "microanalytical underpinning of accelerationism is seriously deficient". He explicates a strong "nonclearing argument" and reveals that "(b)ecause of the absence of market-clearing mechanisms, quantity adjustments carry the burden for many types of product and factor markets, which leads to the observed sluggishness and persistence of inflation and excessive unemployment" (ibid., p 342). As opposed to what he calls "auction markets", an obvious reference to classical Walrasian doctrines, he points to the prevalence of "customer markets" today in key sectors of the economy, where "implicitly contractual long-term relationships" exist "between employees and employers and between customers and suppliers". "By putting price and wage making into a longer-term context, they lengthen the lags and weaken the causal connections between changes in demand and changes in prices or wages." - Okun (1991:342) asserts.

Thus, although "(t)he accelerationist is right that in some respects people are fooled by inflation ... the institutions of the system provide no vehicles of 'unfooling' to transport the economy to a no-tradeoff situation of 'fully anticipated' inflation and a natural unemployment rate" - Okun (ibid., p. 365) concludes.

Heap (1992:20-21) reveals that "in Friedman's analysis ... nominal wages (are) always moving so as to clear the labour market; and so there is never 'unemployment' in his model in the sense of excess supply. The trick as far as employment variation is concerned is that the equilibrium need not occur at the Walrasian full employment value". The "behaviour of participants in labour markets when setting the money wage" depends on "the real wage rate and so ... on expectations about the general level of prices". Thus "when these expectations are wrong the market can equilibrate at a different level of employment" (ibid., p. 21). This can be called "employment variation" with a "slight but significant change in terminology" (ibid., p. 20), actually with an euphemism, we can add, but it is in fact "(disguised unemployment)", Heap says in brackets (ibid., p. 20). To approach it in another way, "when real wages are not determined competitively so as to clear markets, the normative properties of NAIRU cease to be those of full employment ... and we are encouraged to think of forms of supply-side activism" (ibid., pp. 127-128). We can add, putting it simply, that neither under the name of the "natural rate of unemployment" nor under the term NAIRU is this Friedman-Phelps notion identical with full employment; these are arbitrary values that can be situated anywhere along an output axis.

"The nonexistence of the natural rate", as Galbraith and Darity (1994:402) put it, is also realized by "the post-Keynesian perspective", where expectations are considered subjective and being formed by rather volatile processes sometimes nicknamed today by the term 'animal spirits'. This is why there is a "conflict between the post-Keynesian perspective on expectations and that of the new classical economics", which "shows its critical importance to a core proposition, namely whether there can or cannot exist a vertical Phillips curve and a natural rate of unemployment" (ibid.). "If expectations are an independent determining force behind investment and therefore employment, then the concept of a natural rate of unemployment loses its meaning." - Galbraith and Darity (ibid.) say. Then "there is no inherent tendency for the economy to return to any given rate of unemployment once displaced from it (by a shift of expectations). An arbitrary change in expectations can lead to a change in equilibrium unemployment. It thus does not make sense to speak of a natural rate of unemployment." - they add (ibid., p.403).

When they say "equilibrium unemployment" here, it is obviously a kind of 'no tendency to change' type of Marshallian equilibrium, mentioned earlier; that is to say, it does not mean full employment, it can be anywhere along the horizontal output axis. The difference between the Friedman-Phelps "natural rate" hypothesis and the post-Keynesian position is well illustrated in simple price-output figures (ibid., Figure 12.3). As opposed to Friedman's and Phelps's view, who supposed that people were eager to watch the relationship between an expected price level and the actual price level, "(i)t is fruitless to seek an 'objective' expected change in the price level", that kind of objective "information ... does not exist", according to the post-Keynesian view (ibid., p. 404). In consequence there is no natural rate of unemployment and no "natural rate of output", that is, no "output rate that corresponds to the natural rate of employment and unemployment" (ibid., p. 403) in the Friedman-Phelps hypothesis, plotted with vertical lines in figures. In the post-Keynesian view both prices and output may change along a normal, upward sloping aggregate supply curve, and 'no tendency to change' types of equilibria may occur at various levels of unemployment, employment and output.

Indeed, viewing the figures in some books of contemporary mainstream economics, even in works with New Keynesian orientation, one may ask how output can be so much higher than "potential", or, in other words, how such huge parts of the curves can run to the right of the "potential" output points corresponding to "full employment" and the "natural rate of unemployment". In fact the whole way of constructing the aggregate supply curves in these books should be changed. To build up the aggregate supply equations starting from a "natural rate of unemployment" level, that is, from an alleged "full employment" level and a "potential output" level in the middle of the curves and working with the difference between the actual and the asterisk-marked equilibrium-point values is wrong. Such clinging to an equilibrium point is sheer "Classical", that is, Neoclassical economics. Indeed, NKM is in many respects continuing the compromising "Neoclassical Synthesis" of the earlier decades.

It is high time to return to Keynes in earnest and do away with the obligatory equilibrium point, believed in with neoclassical bigotry. Then the right-hand, ascending parts of the aggregate supply curves should not be considered as the province above the equilibrium, above full employment and above potential output, that is, above normality. Then really full employment and "potential", that is, logically, maximum output should be defined in another way and genuinely maximum output should find its right place in the figures: it should be a vertical asymptote approached by the ascending parts, the right-hand, steepening ends, of the aggregate supply curves.

But what about the shape of the long-run Phillips curves, or, put in another way, the long-run aggregate supply curves? Are they not vertical? Indeed, if one examines employment instead of unemployment, then one gets the mirror-image of the curves around a vertical axis, and if one supposes that employment is proportional to output, then one simply gets to the aggregate supply curves within the inflation-output figures. Such aggregate supply curves today, even within the New Keynesian theoretical framework, are often composed directly as expectations-augmented Phillips curves (cf. Dornbusch and Fischer 1990:515-522, 581-582). But then one can rather turn to the good old Keynesian aggregate supply curve of the left-hand (capital letter) L-shape (cf. Hicks 1977:81-84), whether in a prices-output figure or in an inflation-output figure. If the corner of this supply curve is rounded off, approaching the real situation, then one gets something like an approximate mirror-imaged Phillips curve.

Now, if, for instance, by means of Keynesian aggregate demand management, output is increased towards its maximum in the long run, then the final part of this aggregate supply curve, that is, also of the Phillips curve, which is approximately its mirror-image, does indeed turn into a vertical line. Then output is at maximum and only inflation, prices are increasing. But such a phase only ensues when output approaches the technological maximum, the genuine full employment level, and not at some lower output level, defined arbitrarily as the point of the "natural rate" of unemployment, which, as a logical consequence, would have to mean just as arbitrarily "natural" levels of employment and output.

To be correct, it is better to separate the question of the shape of the curves corresponding to higher levels of inflation from the time perspective. Then, without speaking of the "long run", one can see, even by way of another reasoning, that at higher levels of inflation any Phillips curve tends to develop a steep and even backward-leaning shape. Keynes (1936:140-141) writes the following: "Although he does not call it the 'marginal efficiency of capital', Professor Irving Fisher has given in his Theory of Interest (1930) a definition of what he calls 'the rate of return over cost' which is identical with my definition. ... Professor Fisher explains that the extent of investment in any direction will depend on a comparison between the rate of return over cost and the rate of interest. To induce new investment 'the rate of return over cost must exceed the rate of interest. ... Thus Professor Fisher uses his 'rate of return over cost' in the same sense and for precisely the same purpose as I employ 'the marginal efficiency of capital'."

Indeed, whatever one calls the rate of profit on investment, the conclusion is the same as the reasoning which both great scholars of economics, Keynes and Fisher, expressed: the rate of profit should exceed the prevailing interest rate in order to make any investment worthwhile at all. The next question in this theme can be: Which interest rate? Here Fisher's name is especially relevant because he set up the 'Fisher equation' (cf. Fisher 1907; cited by Dornbusch and Fischer 1990:639n), from which we know that the real rate of interest is the nominal rate minus the rate of inflation. But it is not difficult to see that in economic practice it is not the real but the nominal interest rate with which the expected rate of profit on any planned investment has to be compared and which the latter should always exceed in order to be worthwhile.

To see this fact, one can simply think of the possibility that, instead of investing an available sum of money in physical, productive capital and working hard to organize the production of something, one could easily place the money in a bank as a time deposit or could buy bonds for it, without any productive effort. If the expected profit on physical capital, that is to say, on productive investment, is lower than what one can gain after the same period of time from the above-mentioned kinds of financial revenues on the same amount of money at issue, then no one will undertake productive investment. The actual size of the financial revenues mentioned in this comparison, or in another, simple phrase, the cash amounts one gets as interest on deposits, are determined at any time by the nominal rate of interest, which is the sum of the real interest rate and the inflation rate.

The higher the inflation the higher the nominal interest rate, whether on bank deposits or bonds, so the expected profit rate on productive investment has to compete with higher nominal interest rates. If inflation is low, this is not very difficult, but if inflation is high, say, 10, 15, or 20 percent annually, or even higher, then it becomes more and more difficult for any profit on productive investment to keep up with it, even in those cases where the real interest rate diminishes to zero or perhaps becomes negative.

So, if inflation increases, nominal interest rates also increase, and productive investments get into trouble because their profits have to compete with high nominal revenues from easy financial 'investments'. This is why output growth starts to diminish at higher rates of inflation, if we go upwards on the slope of a Phillips curve or on the slope of its approximate mirror image: an aggregate supply curve in an inflation-output figure. Thus the curves at issue become steeper and steeper, close to vertical at higher inflation levels, that is to say, in the long run, if the process continues. Finally the level of output may even decrease at high inflation levels; in other words, the curves may even lean backwards. Such developments also give a logical explanation, among others, to the so-called "stagflation" phenomenon, the simultaneous presence of high inflation and high unemployment in a country. There is no need at all to entertain the "natural rate of unemployment" hypothesis to explain these phenomena.

To sum up: yes, Friedman (1968) was right when he refuted the possibility of forever-lasting, stable trade-offs of "unemployment in exchange for inflation" along one and the same Phillips curve (for that matter, the whole Phillips curve business was not among Keynes's original ideas; it was only adopted during the 1960s by the "Neoclassical Synthesis" brand of Keynesians, in particular by the later Nobel laureates Samuelson and Solow); yes, there can be gradual, adaptive price-rises after a monetary expansion, as described by Friedman (1968:10); yes, the initial and the long-term effects of a monetary expansion can be different, as both Hume (1752a, 1752b) and Friedman (1968) described. However, it is hopeless to suppose that an economy will return to one and the same status quo after several or many years. It is also hopeless to build a theory on highly volatile expectations, and to mistake - under the misleading name of the "natural rate" - high-unemployment disequilibrium situations with "no tendency to change", that is, Marshallian equilibria, for genuine full employment, or even for merely "frictional" or "structural" unemployment.

Friedman's (1968) and Phelps's (1967, 1968) "natural rate of unemployment" hypothesis is an attractive construction of the mind, but it is neither correct in principle nor usable in practice, because it has little to do with reality.

MIXED ECONOMY

All modern economies are in a sense mixed economies, as Sten Johansson (1994a:262) reveals. He characterizes the Swedish 'mixture' as having far-reaching freedom of trading goods, strong consumer control of trade in the housing market, while the service sectors of caring, education and health are to a high degree lifted out from the market. The labour market is strictly regulated by strong, centralized trade unions, there is fairly wide direction of the capital markets, but weak state or collective ownership apart from the publicly directed service sectors, Johansson (ibid.) says.

Indeed, in modern, industrialized countries today we always have to deal with mixed economies. This point can be illustrated briefly with some statistical examples. The first kind of data of interest from this point of view is the proportion of the labour force who work within the public sector. In the United States the proportion of "governmental employment", including federal (civilian), state and local employees, within the "civilian employed labor force" (excluding the unemployed and those "not in the labor force" was about 16.3 percent in 1980 and about 15.6 percent in 1995, according to the U. S. Bureau of the Census (1997:321, 397). The slightly decreasing trend between the figures in this 15-year period might be the result of budget-cutting efforts of right-wing political forces within federal, state and local administrations in this period, which happened to fall under the tide of the historical conservative wave of our age.

As to some roughly corresponding figures for Sweden, for instance, the proportion of "employees in governmental employment" including "state employment" and "local employment" within the "grand total" of all employees was about 41 percent in 1991, about 38.6 percent in 1995 and about 37 percent in 1997, according to Statistics Sweden (1999:177). However, these figures cannot be compared directly with the above figures from the United States because they show the proportion of public sector employees only within the category of all employees, that is, "anställda" in Sweden, and the latter category excludes those who are entrepreneurs or self-employed as well as their helping family-members. If these groups ("företagare") and their helping family-members are also included in the denominator, which means reckoning with all people gainfully employed ("sysselsatta" in Sweden), then the figures are 37.3, 34.3 and 33 percent for 1991, 1995 and 1997, respectively (ibid., pp. 176, 177). The decreasing trend here may mainly be the result of the job-destroying governmental economic policies in Sweden in the early 1990s, affecting the public sector even more heavily than the private sector.

However, according to the data of Olsson and Holmgren (1994:93 Tabell 5.1), the long-term trend is of a strongly increasing character. Incidentally, their data might have been collected with somewhat different classification methods compared to the data of Statistics Sweden (1997). Between 1965 and 1985 the proportion of those working in the public sector within the population of all those gainfully employed ("sysselsatta") had approximately doubled, increasing from 15.3 percent in 1965 to 30.7 percent in 1980; it was 32.7 percent in 1985 and 32.4 percent in 1992 (ibid.). According to Furaker (1987:61), the proportion of public employees within all those who were economically active in Sweden ("förvärvsarbetande") increased from 20.5 percent in 1963 to 38.2 percent in 1985.

Taking a more detailed longer view, Edin and Andersson (1995:11) reveal that in Sweden "(t)he greatest expansion of the public sector took place during the 1960s and '70s". In a relative sense "the expansion of the public sector came to a halt during the 1980s", but in spite of this, "as a portion of the total work force, Sweden has the world's largest public sector" (ibid.). As regards some interesting further characteristics of Swedish conditions, as Edin and Andersson (ibid.) say, "it is also true that a much larger portion of Sweden's population participates in the (total) work force, due to the high percentage of women employed in the public sector. ... In Sweden, 78 percent of adult women participate in the work force, as opposed to only 61 percent in the European Union as a whole. The difference of 17 percent is accounted for by women working in the Swedish public sector. That the Swedish public sector is so large is both a precondition and a consequence of women's high employment frequency", Edin and Andersson conclude. Nevertheless, they also point out that in Sweden "the expansion of the female-dominated public sector has hardly been a hindrance to the male-dominated private sector. ... A comparison of the number of employees (excluding the self-employed) in relation to the total work force reveals that Sweden has the highest level of private sector employment in all of Europe" as well (ibid., p. 12).

Another, even more favoured way of looking at the mixed character of the economy is the examination of the size of all government spending as the proportion of GDP or GNP. As regards some data about the United States, in 1996 "government consumption expenditures and gross investment" including federal, state and local figures were 1406.4 billion USD, and this represented 18.56 percent of GDP, according to the U. S. Bureau of the Census (1997:447). In the same year "government transfer payments to persons" amounted to 1056.7 billion USD, which meant around 13.95 percent of GDP. Adding this to the sum of government expenditure and investment above, the total government spending amounted to 2463.1 billion USD in 1996, which represented about 32.5 percent of GDP (ibid., p. 452). This can by and large be compared with the figures quoted by Gregory and Ruffin (1994:73, Exhibit 1), who say that in 1991 "Total Expenditures for Goods and Services and Transfers" for "Federal" and "State and local" governments together in the United States were 1907 billion USD, which represented 33.4 percent of GDP.

On the same page Gregory and Ruffin (ibid., Exhibit 2) show a historical comparison for several countries in respect of "the general increase in government spending as a percentage of total economic activity" between 1890 and 1991. The lines drawn for six countries show that in all of them "the government's share of economic activity has been rising over the long run" (ibid., p. 74), and, except for Japan and Germany, this has been the case continually, for all the decades covered by the figure. It is interesting to observe the fact that among the six countries shown in the exhibit, at the final point of the examined period: in 1991 the United States had the lowest size of "Total Government Spending as a Percentage of GDP", a little over 30 percent, more exactly 33.4 percent, as we have seen, while Sweden had far the highest size, well over 60 percent. The U. K., France and Germany had corresponding figures of around 50 percent and Japan of around 36 percent in 1991.

As regards a wider group of countries for a comparison, Edin and Andersson (1995:11, Figure 13) after Korpi and Palme (1993:164) show the proportion of "Social Transfer Payments & Public Sector Expenditures as % of GDP" for Sweden and 17 OECD countries in 1989. Concerning the proportion of transfer payments alone, Sweden was that time surpassed by the Netherlands, Belgium and even France (about 1985 cf. also Korpi and Palme 1998:675), but in respect of the sum of all public expenditures and transfer payments together Sweden had the largest proportion of GDP in 1989, about 46 percent.

This figure, the size of total government spending as the percentage of GDP, seems to be fairly interesting from the view-point of various types of economic and/or political comparisons; the question is worth a closer examination, starting with Sweden. As Olsson and Oberkofler (1994:30, Tabell 4.1) show, the proportion of the total outlays of the public sector in Sweden, calculated as "brutto", that is to say, gross, including all direct taxes, and calculating at "market prices", that is to say, prices including all indirect taxes, was 71.7 percent of BNP in 1993. However, as Ehrenberg (1996:66-68) also indicated and Olsson and Oberkofler (1994:9-24) explain in detail, this high gross figure is somewhat misleading in international comparisons because transfer payments in Sweden are subject to direct taxation and the total transfer outlays always include these taxes too. In other words, they are calculated with the gross amounts the beneficiaries receive, before paying their income taxes, which taxes are later paid back into the public sector budgets. Calculated with the deduction of these returned amounts of direct taxes, but still at market prices, the netto total outlays of the public sector in Sweden were only 56.5 percent of BNP in 1993 (ibid., p. 34, Tabell 4.4).

Some international comparisons including six European countries are also made by Olsson and Oberkofler (ibid., p. 36) for the year 1990, which show that calculating the total outlays of the public sector in gross and with market prices, Sweden had the highest level with 61 percent of BNP in 1990, followed by Denmark with 59 percent and the Netherlands with 57.8 percent of BNP. However, calculating in "netto", that is to say, net amounts, deducing the direct taxes on the transfers, and with "factor prices", that is, deducing the indirect taxes, Denmark has the highest proportion of public outlays with 53.9 percent of BNP, followed by the Netherlands with 53.4 percent, and Sweden was only in third place with 53.1 percent of BNP. Germany also had almost as high a proportion of public outlays as the above countries: it had 49.5 percent, while Norway had only 45.9 percent and Great Britain 45.4 percent of BNP in 1990, according to the latter type of calculation.

One can conclude that the differences between the modern European countries are not very large in this respect; all of them have their total public sector outlays around 50 percent of their BNPs with the latter type of calculation. In other words, their public sectors spend in one way or another about half of the yearly revenue of the country. This is a convincing proof of the fact that all modern countries have mixed economies, as Johansson (1994a:262) pointed out.

As regards the rate of change during the past decades in the case of Sweden, Furaker (1987:53) points out that the size of public sector outlays as a proportion of BNP increased from 25 percent in 1950 to 67.1 percent in 1983.

Olsson and Oberkofler (1994:29-31, 33-34, 41) also have time series data for Sweden and five other European countries, which show that their total public sector outlays as well as the transfers to households within them have mostly been on the increase in recent decades. This experience agrees well with the long-time pattern shown earlier by Gregory and Ruffin (1994:73, Exhibit 2). So, as time goes by, the modern countries can less and less be regarded as having the features of pure market economies and should be considered as having more and more of the characteristics of mixed economies.

An important question that occurs rather frequently in economic and political debates is the so-called "burden of maintenance" of the giant and still growing public sector. A favourite topic of conservatively oriented disputants is the heavy burden of maintaining the whole public sector allegedly weighing down the private sector. In connection with this problem it is interesting to read Olsson's and Holmgren's (1994:79, Tabell 2.1) data, who reveal that in Sweden the proportion of those people within the total population who were actually at work decreased from 42.7 percent in 1965 to a mere 39 percent in 1992.

Further analysing the majority 61 percent who were not at work in Sweden in 1992, Olsson and Holmgren (ibid., p. 80, Tabell 2.2) point out that the proportion of those people who did not have any revenue of their own decreased from about 38 percent of the total population in 1965 to about 26 percent in 1992. The main reasons for this change were the growing proportion of women who entered the labour force as opposed to being dependent housewives as earlier, as well as the decreasing number of dependent children. In addition to the 26 percent who were still dependants in 1992, about 10 percent of the population, also within the 61 percent not at work, were away from their work only temporarily; they were, for instance, on holiday, working for their trade union, on sick-pay, parental leave, or partial pension, etc. The remaining, approximately 25 percent of the population, also within the 61 percent not at work, were those who had their own revenue because they lived on various transfers, for example, preliminary or old-age pension, unemployment benefit, etc. For that matter, the proportion of transfers within the total revenue of all households is fairly high in Sweden; in 1992 about 38 percent of the total after-tax income of all households came from various transfers, according to Olsson and Holmgren (ibid., p. 84).

These facts gradually lead us to the core of the above-mentioned main question of who maintains whom in society, on the basis of the

Swedish example. Olsson and Holmgren (1994:95) cite an allegation in a radio broadcast that 70 percent of the population is maintained by the mere 30 percent left, via the public sector. On the basis of the data presented by Olsson and Holmgren (ibid., p. 79, Tabell 2.1 and p. 93, Tabell 5.1) these figures might even be sharper. According to the data presented, in 1992 only 39 percent of the population were at work, and if we suppose that their distribution between the public and the private sectors were the same as that of all who were gainfully employed ("sysselsatta" in Swedish), then 67.6 of them worked in the private sector. This means that only about 26 percent of the total population were at work in the private sector in 1992, the others being either out of work or at work in the public sector. Since the public sector as a whole is supposed to be maintained by tax revenues, it is easy for populist conservative arguments to spread the belief that it is also "maintained" by the private sector. This would mean that a mere 26 percent of the population "maintains" the 74 percent, including among others both public welfare beneficiaries and public sector employees (as well as their dependants).

Allegations that the public sector is "maintained" by the private sector often imply that the public sector employees are some kind of parasites, who sponge on the market economy, on the honest private sector. This would mean that most doctors, nurses, social workers, teachers, etc. are parasites, who sponge on the only really important, normal, basic sector, on the real heroes of the market economy, say, a boy distributing leaflets in the street about a new hair-dye at a private perfumery.

A better way of seeing society as a whole may well be the following: all people have their place in the system of social division of labour, including those not at work at any time due to young or old age, state of health, dependent status, education, holiday, etc. Many of those at work do their job within the public sector, other groups do so within the private sector, and if one adds up those actually at work in the latter, it turns out that they are in a minority. This fact in itself does not mean any kind of evaluation about importance or its negation. Only a tiny fragment of the labour force in modern societies, about 3 percent in both Sweden and the

United States, work in agriculture (cf. Statistics Sweden 1999:175, Tab. 200 and U. S. Bureau of the Census 1997:415, No. 649), and their proportions within the total population is still lower, but they "feed" the whole country. There are many professions whose activities are important in society, both in the public and the private sectors, and it makes no sense to speak about "maintenance" in a pejorative sense, either according to professions or sectors.

So, allegations about the 26 percent "maintaining" the 74 percent somewhat resemble a claim that in a modern industrialized country the 3 percent of the labour force working in agriculture "maintain" the 97 percent, because they are those actually producing the food. "We keep them all alive" - the agricultural workers could say in this sense. As opposed to such kinds of allegations, the reality is what Olsson and Holmgren (ibid., pp. 92, 96) explain, namely the fact that public sector employees are not "maintained" by private sector employees, but they simply do other kinds of working tasks which society as a whole needs. It is only the particular characteristics of the payment system of society which are arranged so that the public sector is formally "financed" mostly by taxes, or at least it seems so. For that matter, as Berglund (1996:89) asserts, in effect the public sector is not really financed by taxes and other public revenues; the real purpose of all public revenues is only to draw in private purchasing power.

One can add that in a little more abstract sense all private sector employees are also maintained by "taxes", only the name of these "taxes" and the ways of collecting them are different. Instead of universal direct or indirect taxes, the latter being a component of prices anyway, the private sector "taxes" can be called, for instance, the wage-cost component of prices, collected through the turnover returns of the private companies. In other words, they are imposed on and collected from some special groups of ad hoc tax-subjects: the customers.

Thus the truth in the above Swedish example is simply that in 1992 the 39 percent of the population who were at work, according to Olsson and Holmgren (1994:79, Tabell 2.1), in the public and the private sectors together, by and large "maintained" the whole population, including the 61 percent not at work, of which 10 percent were temporarily absent, about 25.3 percent lived on various transfers, and about 25.7 percent were dependants (ibid., p. 80, Tabell 2.2). We say by and large "maintained" because even many of those people officially within the 61 percent not at work in effect did a considerable amount of productive, that is to say, useful working activities. We refer primarily not to the so-called black economy, but to the huge amount of housework, hobby work, voluntary work, which is done every day in most households and by many people, and which is usually not (yet) accounted for within the discipline of economics today.

There is no doubt that all modern countries are very far from what could be considered a pure or even an approximately pure market economy. Like it or not, they are already rather mixed economies today. If we took the liberty to ironize a little, we could ask whether the conservatively oriented trends of economics argue so desperately for the cutting back of the public sector precisely in order not to disturb their pure market theories and to retain or restore their old world where the laws of the market could still be regarded as unconditionally valid. To top it all, apart from temporary changes due to rightist political and restrictive economic courses, and despite the deliberate efforts of such regimes in power to cut back the public sector from time to time, the long-term historical trend seems to be the gradual, slow increase of the size and weight of the public sector within the economies of most modern countries.

Instead of the zealous but in the long run vain striving of conservative forces to push back and diminish the public sector at any cost, the main question in our age and in the future is to find the "right" or "best" mixture of the mixed economy for every country. This optimal mixture will obviously lie somewhere between the two theoretical extremes of a pure market economy model and a state-run economy model. The term "right" or "best" mixture could mean a welfare regime, to use a term borrowed from Esping-Andersen (1996, 1999), which provides favourable, humane conditions of life for the whole population, and in terms of economic parameters provides low unemployment with low, bearable inflation, for a fairly long period of time. As regards economic growth, which is the most frequent third main criterion for economists to judge the performance of an economy, the interests of economic growth should always be carefully balanced against the interests of preservation of the environment. To achieve the above-mentioned goals, the decreasing of unemployment in particular, it seems that in most modern countries a controlled increase of the public sector has an important role to play. In sharp contrast with the usual contemporary advice of conservative economists, a somewhat greater public sector activity in the form of a 'combined Keynesian expansion', specifically in creating welfare service types of jobs, financed by monetization, that is, newly created money, can be beneficial in the future. We will expound these suggestions in the coming chapters.

At this point I wish to mention a friendly suggestion of a colleague, Mats Benner, who, after reading the manuscript, proposed including here an analysis of the voluminous literature dealing with the development of the mixed economy in the advanced societies since the Second World War. He suggested including, for instance, such prominent authors as Shonfield (1965, cf. also 1984, a posthumus work), Scharpf (1991), Jessop (cf. 1990), Streeck (cf. 1992), Crouch (cf. 1993), Boyer (cf. 1990), as well as those authors analysing the most recent developments connected with the concept of the mixed economy, for example, Pedersen et al. (cf. 1992), Nielsen and Pedersen (cf. 1990), and also the effects of globalization, for instance, Kitschelt et al. (1997).

At the same time I reveal that the way the notion of the mixed economy is tackled here, in terms of the relative size of the public sector, is a simplified presentation. As, for instance, Shonfield (1984:4) points out, "the degree of 'mixedness' is not determined by the size of the public sector or the proportion of public expenditure to the national income" alone. In his opinion "(i)t is the function adopted by the state rather than its mass which counts" (ibid.). Shonfield is perfectly right and so are Matzner and Streeck (1991:9) when they explain that an "advanced post-Keynesian employment policy" must be far wider today than "the type of demand management that is usually associated with Keynesianism". Public intervention and regulation of various kinds are vital components of mixed economies, but since my aim in the present work is to question some fundamental dogmas of conservative economics, as well as to raise just a few ideas in order to progress towards finding some solutions to the problems of underemployment and deteriorating welfare services, I postpone reviewing complex theories of state intervention and regulation.

Indeed, a detailed, systematic review of all such theories which can be characterized as watching and analysing "modern capitalism", naturally included, for instance, Bottomore (1985), who (ibid., p. 3) even gives a concise history of the term "capitalism", and among others Benner (1997), one of the most recent contributions, is a tempting proposal, but it needs a considerably longer, complete research agenda. Unfortunately, time is running out for me right now, because one of the purposes of the present work is to contribute to a quick intellectual rebellion against the prevalent rule of conservative economics as much time in advance as possible before the scheduled hurried completion of the EMU project on 1 January 2002 and before crucial plebiscites about the EMU in several European countries. I am very grateful for Benner's suggestion, and I will be happy to progress to such a detailed future research program, hopefully leading to a concluding subsequent volume under the preliminary working title "Mixed Economies in Modern Capitalism".

WELFARE SERVICES

As regards the future spectrum of occupations in the advanced Western societies, it is well-known today that the proportion of manpower employed in the goods-producing sectors of the economy (except in information technology production branches) is generally decreasing and the proportion of those employed in various kinds of services is increasing.

In the economy of the United States in 1996 the proportions of the main sectors were as follows: those working in the primary sector, that is, agriculture, within the "total employed" was 2.7 percent, those working in the secondary, that is, the industrial sector, was about 23 percent, and the rest, about 74.3 percent, were working in various kinds of services, in other words, in the tertiary or service sector. Although the classifications within the service sector were multifarious and in places the sub-categories were not shown separately, two broad categories can by and large be distinguished. The proportion of those kinds of services connected with business and trade, including transport and communication, etc. amounted to about 44 percent of the "total employed", and the proportion of those kinds of services which include health care, education, social services, as well as cultural services and public administration, etc. amounted to about 30 percent of the approximately 126.7 million of "total employed" in 1996, according to the U. S. Bureau of the Census (1997:415, table No. 649).

Some generally corresponding figures for Sweden in 1997 were as follows: the primary or agricultural sector, including forestry and fishing, occupied about 2.78 percent of all those gainfully employed ("sysselsatta"), the secondary, industrial sector occupied about 26 percent, and the rest, about 71.2 percent worked in the tertiary, that is, the service sector. This distribution is fairly similar to that of the United States a year earlier, in 1996. As to the further distribution of the service sector, it is not easy to determine the details of sub-classification here either, but it seems that the sizes of the two broad categories mentioned above proved to be the other way round in Sweden. The proportion of those services connected with business and trade, including communication, etc., amounted to about 31 percent, while the proportion of those kinds of services which include health care, sanitation, education, social work, personal services, cultural activities, as well as public administration, amounted to about 40 percent of all those gainfully employed in 1997, according to Statistics Sweden (1999:175, Tab. 200).

Thus the ratio of "business services" to "humanitarian" or "humane" types of services in the United States in 1996 was about 44 percent to 30 percent, while in Sweden in 1997 it was more or less vice versa: about 31 percent to 40 percent, clearly in favour of the "humane" types of services.

The directions of change of the three main sectors of the economy in modern, industrialized countries are well-known today, and they are congruent with what had been predicted a few decades earlier (cf., for instance, Dombos 1979). Some statistics today even make detailed forecasts about the growth tendencies of various occupations (cf. U. S. Bureau of the Census 1997:393, 414-416).

It turns out from these forecasts that the proportions of two groups of services are particularly likely to increase fastest in the future, those involving the operation of information technology (IT) on the one hand, and those which can be called welfare services or personal services (cf. Halmos 1970) on the other hand.

As to the first group, typical kinds of occupations whose

proportions are definitely on the increase today are, for instance, those connected with the repair, programming or consultations regarding computers. The proportion of such kinds of jobs may increase in both the private and the public sectors in the short and medium-term. However, in a decade or two, like a possible saturation of the market in advanced countries with IT products, the proportion of new "IT application" types of jobs may also begin to grow less steeply and approach their limits.

The second group of rapidly increasing service occupations in modern societies, those belonging to what can be called the "humane services", welfare services or personal services types of jobs, are more independent of technological booms. In broad terms they can be summed up as involving all kinds of care for the young, the old and the sick. Thus whole provinces of the public services, the education system, the health service, the care of young children, the care of old people, all belong to this branch of occupations.

Halmos (1970) spoke of these kinds of jobs as the "helping professions" (ibid., p.3) or as the "personal service professions" (ibid., p. 22 ff), mentioning "the clergy, doctors, nurses, teachers, social workers, to list only the largest groups" (ibid., p. 22). He asserted that "those professions which I have called the 'personal service professions', having already dramatically grown in numbers, will go on growing and proliferating in the coming decades" (ibid., p. 25). He proved the validity of this statement with statistical data, and he predicted that the spirit of the personal service professions would also eventually influence and pervade the minds of what he called the "impersonal service professionals", that is to say, people working in the other intellectual professions (ibid., pp. 25-62).

Halmos (1970:55) pointed out the problem of "professional manpower shortage, already in evidence for some time, and showing every sign of becoming more acute with every extension of service in the areas of health, welfare, and education". But, as Halmos (ibid.) says, this will also mean a great number of new job possibilities. He says that "Martin Luther King's book, Where Do We Go From Here?, is quoted as saying that the expansion of human service industry is going to be the 'missing industry' which will 'soak up the unemployment that persists in the US'". He also cites Pearl and Riessman (1965), who "propose 'that human service occupations can be re-organized to produce better services by allowing disadvantaged, undereducated people to produce useful work at new entry-level jobs with training and education built-in ...'" (ibid.).

Halmos (ibid., pp. 9-10) aptly described the changing character of economic tasks in advanced societies, away from goods-production and towards the production of more services, as well as the influence of these changes on both the character and the required number of jobs: "The medium of achievement in an increasingly professionalised society is increasingly the 'services rendered' and decreasingly the 'goods provided'. In an increasingly affluent and technologically developed society the intelligent and educated manpower required to furnish the goods will be more and more rationalised and limited, while the manpower required to render personal services in health, welfare, and education need have no bounds.". A similar idea is expressed by Gran (1997:308) when he says that "history suggests the value of ensuring the welfare of entire populations. A longer time-frame indicates that a strong welfare state contributes not only to the health of civil and political components of societies, but also to their economies.".

As regards some actual recent data about the frequency of "personal service" types of jobs, which we could call welfare occupations or welfare service occupations, in the United States in 1995 about 58 percent of all government employees, including federal, state and local levels and both full-time and part-time employment, had these occupations, according to the U. S. Bureau of the Census (1997:321, table No. 507). A roughly comparable figure for Sweden in 1996 is about 76.55 percent of all public sector employees, who worked in the fields of education, research, health care, religion, culture, recreation, sports, and other similar service activities, according to Statistics Sweden (1999:178-179, 193-194, Tab. 205, 206 with data for early 1998, 215).

It is interesting to see how the percentage of women in the labour force, that is, the proportion of female employment within the population, has increased and is still increasing from decade to decade in modern countries, in close connection with the growing significance and number of welfare service occupations. In the case of the United States this is shown by the U. S. Bureau of the Census (1997:397-400, table Nos. 619-624). As regards Sweden, it is well-known that the degree of participation of women in the labour force is one of the highest among all countries in the world in recent decades; however, in the last few years, from the early 1990s onwards, these figures have decreased somewhat (cf., for instance, Statistics Sweden 1999:174-175, Tab. 197-199). This is closely connected with a similar decrease of the number of employees in welfare service occupations, in precisely the same years, from the early 1990s onwards, according to Statistics Sweden (1999:175, Tab. 200).

The cause of these phenomena lies hidden in wrong economic policies pursued in Sweden, to some extent, for instance, with financial deregulation, already starting in the late 1980s, but particularly worsening from the early 1990s onwards. This led to several years of economic recession in the first half of the 1990s and started to erode what has been generally regarded for many decades as the "Swedish model", the "prototype" of the welfare state and thus "of modern society" (cf. Tomasson 1970) (cf. also Edin and Carlsson 1995:9-15; Andersson 1998:8).

On the basis of the bad Swedish example of the early 1990s, the complaint of the Memorandum (1998:11) is quite justified about contemporary attempts to carry out "a substantial shrinking of the welfare state" and a "subordination of large parts of the traditional welfare system to the rules of private profit". Opposing these attempts a renewed emphasis on "individual and collective welfare objectives" and on the "values of solidarity, equity and ecological sustainability" is indeed necessary (ibid., p. 8).

According to Ahrne (1998a:165), "(i)n democratic welfare states ... social services are usually associated with the idea of social rights". Referring to Marshall (1965) he reveals that after civil rights and political rights, "(s)ocial rights are the last and the least developed forms of citizenship rights that have evolved in democratic states", and that "unlike civil and political rights social rights are based on scarce resources". In consequence, Ahrne (ibid.) concludes, "social rights are" exposed to "shifts in the economic situation of the state and they are objects of political struggles and compromises". So are the actual conditions of providing or not providing various particular kinds of social services, or in our terminology 'welfare services', to the citizens of any country, we can add.

A heated debate is going on in advanced societies today about the extent to which these services should be supplied by public versus private institutions and arrangements, or possibly still by the oldest, traditional source of these caring functions in society: the family.

To begin with the last alternative, we cannot deal now with the economic role of such arrangements within the family. They are difficult to grasp with the present conceptual tools of economics, even though there already exist attempts to develop certain kinds of assessments to examine the equivalent values of unpaid work performed within households. Such assessments could probably be most useful for some kind of a more collectivistic family-type in the more distant (or perhaps not so distant) future, so much the more so because in our age the contemporary types of family in our advanced Western society are all in deep crisis and in the process of dissolution.

In the West the traditional, extended family type for the most part already belongs to the past, to the Victorian times, for instance. It is still prevalent, though, in the developing world. But the comparatively new type of family that gradually ousted and replaced it in our modern Western society during the course of the 20th century, and which is most often today called the nuclear family, still prevalent even recently, is already under dissolution, too, here and now, before our eyes. The proportion of both one-person households and one-parent families is on the increase rapidly, while the proportion of official marriages is decreasing quickly, being replaced by longer or shorter periods of cohabitation, if at all.

The crisis and dissolution of the contemporary types of family in our advanced Western society is one reason why more and more welfare service or personal service types of jobs will be needed here in the course of time. The care of the young, the old and the sick can be provided for to an ever-decreasing extent within family frameworks, hence growing branches of the economy are needed to provide for them. Another reason is the ongoing change in the demographic composition of the population in our advanced industrial countries. Fortunately, as a result of higher standards of living, life expectancy is generally rising. This favourable phenomenon has led to the need for more and more or the labour force to be employed in the care of the old and the sick. In numerous Western countries there is already a shortage of health service personnel, and this is closely connected with the problem of financing the institutions of the public health service.

The care of the young and the education sector as a whole also suffer from labour shortage in many Western countries, as more and more women enter the labour market, and as the significance of education, together with the number of years spent by young people in educational institutions, is growing. Such labour shortages are perpetuated by the fact that in personal service jobs there is comparatively little room for productivity increases due to technological development. For instance, computers may have some subsidiary roles to play in these fields, but as regards the main working tasks in personal services in general, there is little room for mechanization, let alone automation. Low productivity means little prospect for 'rationalizing' away the numbers of personnel, hence there is a lasting and even growing need for manpower. In these humanitarian fields the viewpoints of economic efficiency must be reduced to a lower rank in importance, and priority must be given to the quality of the services. Even the second rank in importance should be given to the provision of job opportunities here, also before economic efficiency.

As Gustafsson (1995:98) points out, if and when decisions in the field of social policy are made based on the efficiency criterion of the market economy, that would cause a detrimental change of purpose in the whole system of the welfare state. Any striving after direct economic efficiency in the field of welfare services can easily lead to inhumane, even dangerous conditions. More primitive societal arrangements can be mentioned as analogies in this question; for instance, some ancient tribes allegedly left their aged family members without care, to die alone, in order to economize, or another, contemporary example: child labour, instead of education, is rather widespread in some developing countries even today. As opposed to any striving after direct economic efficiency on the spot, for human society as a whole economic efficiency on a universal scale and in the long run is best served by always focusing in welfare services on the final goal: the welfare of people.

In the current state of affairs in our Western societies it seems that the welfare or personal service branches of the economy are not going to be threatened by any kind of actual saturation in job needs or job opportunities in the foreseeable future, provided the question of financing can be solved. At present we are still far from the limits in improving the proportion of the personnel employed to provide the needed services relative to the number of recipients, which, in other words, in fact means improving the quality of the services, if sufficient financial resources could somehow be created.

Indeed, as among others, for example, Dombos (1979) predicted, and as some contemporary statistical figures mentioned above also illustrated, the goods-producing sectors of the economy are on a long, historical trend of decrease as regards the proportion of the total labour force working within them. In consequence new jobs in greater numbers can only be hoped to be generated within the tertiary, that is, the service sector. The next question is: in what kind of services can new jobs be generated? Within the "business" types of private services technological improvements, in particular the current spreading of IT, that is, information technology, most often mean today that jobs are rationalized away rapidly. The consequence is rather frequently that more investment produces a smaller increase or even causes a decrease in the number of employment opportunities. On the other hand, in the "humane", welfare types of services the numbers of both new and old jobs needed are much less threatened by technological development, and in consequence these services constitute great reserves for job creation in the future. If such job creation is carried out, it means a further advantage for society, in addition to providing better care for the needs of people.

As Esping-Andersen (1996a:11) and Stephens (1996:35) show, the Scandinavian welfare states have already begun progressing in this direction both as regards welfare expenditures within GDP and the proportion of welfare types of jobs. As Stephens (ibid.) says, "... the Scandinavian welfare states are (distinctive) in terms of the expansion of public social services". As a result, already "in the mid 1980s, welfare state employment (i.e. public health, education, and welfare employment) accounted for an average of 15.4 per cent of the working age population in the four Scandinavian countries ...". According to Esping-Andersen (1996b:72), "(i)n Denmark and Sweden, public sector employment in health, education and welfare services reached 25 per cent of the labour force in the late 1980s, compared with a range of 6-11 per cent in continental Europe ...(Esping-Andersen, 1990:158)".

To create new jobs mainly in welfare services, that is, in what Ehrenberg (1996:144) calls the human sector ("den mänskliga sektorn"), is also the best from an ecological point of view, because it means non-material growth. We should accept Boulding's (1968) analogy about the Earth as a "living spaceship with a finely balanced life-support system", cited by Korten (1995:25), because the environment and the natural resources should indeed be carefully economized with in the long run. From this point of view growth in the welfare services is the best kind of economic growth because people's caring for each other usually does not endanger the environment and does not consume much of the scarce energy resources.

As regards a practical objection according to which some groups of the unemployed may be reluctant to undertake welfare service types of jobs because of their unpleasant characteristics, the solution may be to raise the level of remuneration in welfare service jobs with unpleasant traits or conditions.

As to the main and most frequent question in contemporary debates: whether public or private arrangements should provide for welfare or personal services in our advanced Western society, a general answer can run as follows: both, but the basic, main services should be provided for by the public sector.

The explanation of such a standpoint of proposing "mixed" welfare services can be based on various arguments which in part contrast with each other, so a careful balance between public and private arrangements should be worked out in each country and regarding each particular type of service at issue.

According to Berglund (1996:84), from a purely economic point of view it is wrong to place public and private activities in sharp contrast with each other, because an increase in public activities most often leads to an even greater increase in demand in the private sector. But even from the view-point of the quality of the services rendered it is also necessary to have an "interplay between public and private institutions when it comes to providing welfare", as Erikson et al. (1987:ix) put it. "The analysis suggests that the private and public sectors are not antagonistic but instead support each other in providing care and services for the dependents in society." - they reveal (ibid.).

The comprehensive quantitative priority that should be given to the public services can be explained by the principle of universalism. A general coverage of the whole population, including even the poorest, neediest people, is undoubtedly necessary as an elementary requirement in a modern society. Such comprehensive public arrangements also have the advantage of promoting the great social value of equality. A minimum level of necessary services, whether in education, health care, baby-care or care of the aged, should be provided to each and every individual from cradle to grave, as a fundamental right.

As Erikson et al. (1987:vii-viii) put it, "free or cheap education for all (is preferred) in publicly owned educational institutions with a standard sufficiently high to discourage the demand for private schooling; free or cheap health care on the same basis ... Transfers and services are regarded as a right for all rather than a charity for the needy." Welfare services left merely to charity or churches would indeed be extremely meagre and would perpetuate widespread poverty similar to the conditions of early capitalism in the 18th and 19th centuries, one can add.

Sweden, the "Swedish model" can and should invariably be referred to as a positive example in this respect. As Johansson (1994a:278, Note 13.) reveals, much of the good characteristics of Sweden are not included in the dry figures of BNP when one third of the economy is driven without profit purpose. The "value" of the fact that all people have good housing and that health services, care and education are available for all, generally cannot be calculated in figures.

However, the public sector's providence of the general, basic level and type of welfare services should be supplemented in every country with various kinds of private alternatives. The main purpose of these private alternatives is to provide for the possibility of choice, and thus to break any inclinations or their vestiges here and there for contingent bureaucratic abuse of office, power, position in possibly surviving post-feudalistic, monopolistic structures. The possibility of choice is important in order to make the "ofrivilliga passagerarna", as Ahrne (1997, cf. p. 20) calls them, that is, the "involuntary passengers" in the prescribed, strait "journeys" of the welfare state, feel less compulsion and be less involuntary and happier (cf. also Ahrne 1998b:143).

Nevertheless, the size and proportion of the private arrangements in providing for full coverage of a particular service for the whole population should not be too large. While a main fault in public services might be the exposure of the recipient to arbitrary, monopolistic, bureaucratic power, on the other hand, in private services the recipients might be exposed to the hidden detriments of greedy financial motivations of the providers of services. In many private arrangements the recipients, whether in education or the health service or elsewhere, are often or even usually not in the position of being able to evaluate objectively whether the quality of the service is in correct proportion to the price, and furthermore, whether a particular part of the service is necessary or not. This is why any analogy referring to the restaurant and hotel industry by conservatively oriented thinkers is misconceived. The users of the latter kinds of services are mostly able to control the relationship between quality and price, as well as the necessity of the parts of the services they order.

However, as Ahrne et al. (1996:156) point out, after Persson (1980) and Rombach (1994), this is typically not the case when it comes to education and health care services. Here the chances that the customers can themselves judge and compare the quality of services and without any great risk shop around and try various producers or sellers, so that a wrong judgement does not lead to serious, irreparable negative consequences, are rather limited. Market-type arrangements presuppose strong and well-informed customers in possession of a thorough knowledge of the field. This is often or even usually not the case concerning welfare services, one can conclude.

But even apart from the "humane" types of services, privatization may often prove harmful in other types of services, for instance, in the comprehensive systems belonging to the "infrastructure" of a country. Transport and communication may produce typical examples. The root cause of the death of all the victims who died in the horrible train catastrophe at the outskirts of London in early October 1999 may be summed up in one word: privatization. Or in a few words: the pursuit of private profit. As the investigation showed, the profit interests of the private companies were in direct conflict with the interests of greater safety.

As regards the field of education, it is well-known that private arrangements based on the market often lead to contraselection in favour of those less talented students who have a more well-to-do family background, and thus perpetuate social inequality. In contrast, public systems with free education provide equal chances for all talented students and foster social equality. The question of equality is very important in education. As Erikson and Jonsson (1996a:2) say: "Social selection in schools leads to reduced social efficiency since it means a waste of talent." Besides, "(t)he fact that children from the lower classes are given less opportunity to develop their intellectual capacities must be regarded as a major injustice". As Erikson and Jonsson (1996b:65) reveal in another essay, the problem is not even new, because "(l)iberal claims for equality of opportunity were made by the political left in the late 19th century. It was considered a grave injustice that a person's life chances should be dependent upon circumstances to which she was born."

As regards services in health care, to borrow the words of Erikson (1992:218), here it is also important "... to reduce differences in health between different groups in the ... population". According to Vagerö (1995:1), "the reduction of health inequalities may represent a great potential for improving the health of the population"; however, besides this, "there is a moral justification for equal distribution of health risks and health resources even if this did not contribute greatly to improved general health". In another work Vagerö (1994:1203) sums up that "(t)he reduction of inequalities in health can be seen as an overall strategy for the improvement of a population's health, and as helpful in the maintaining and improvement of its human capital".

The health service is usually a fairly sensitive topic for people and a favourite topic of the debates about the vice and virtues of public versus private arrangements, so some kinds of typical faults in these two contrasting systems can perhaps be illustrated in this area. In the public health system a typical fault might be the neglect of services or careless treatment. Since the staff get a permanent salary from the public sector, if they are egoistic and not conscientious enough, their self-interest might manifest itself in doing less work for the same salary. In private health services the opposite kind of fault might typically occur: the overdoing of services, providing treatment even unnecessarily, being driven by financial motivation. According to the old saying, you can go into some private hospitals to have a corn removed from your foot and come out with one leg amputated. To make the salary of any health staff sharply dependent on "achievement", in a good capitalist spirit, for instance, on the number and size of operations, might in some cases be life-endangering.

Perhaps the above reasoning about the strong financial motives of private health care will elicit the protest of devoted physicians, who might feel such suspicions to be cynical. Fortunately, many or perhaps most employees in the health services of modern countries can well be supposed to be driven primarily by humanitarian motives and the sense of duty. Nevertheless, the motivations within the souls of human beings are very complex, and financial motives, working even subconsciously, may play the greater role for individuals the greater emphasis they receive in the profession at issue, and even in society and the economy as a whole, in particular if the economy is vigorously promoted to have and actually pushed into having more and more "market economy" characteristics.

Private institutional arrangements in health care, as well as in other kinds of services, may play important supplementary roles, but the basic systems of welfare or personal services should generally be based on the public sector, with a careful balance between public and private arrangements, and possibly combined arrangements, being worked out everywhere.

THE PUBLIC SECTOR AS REMEDY

By further developing public welfare services, instead of cutting them down as the prevailing conservative trends of macroeconomics suggest in most advanced Western countries, the role of the public sector in the economy, already sizable enough, will naturally increase further. This means that the already mixed character of the economy that these countries de facto have today, as opposed to the frequent theoretical illusion of having a pure market economy, will become even more mixed, and the "market laws" cannot be as valid as, for instance, the monetarists believe they are. The even greater role the public sector is coming to play will be on the whole beneficial.

Taking the contemporary West-European countries in general and Scandinavian countries in particular as starting points, it seems that a little larger public sector with support given to necessary welfare service types of jobs, financed by monetization, that is to say, newly created money, can be an appropriate way today in the search for the best mixtures for our economies. Besides that, public sector job creation may get on the historical agenda again as a solution in the early years of the third millenium if, in the wake of the recent and perhaps renewed South-East Asian and Russian, and also possible Latin-American crises, a new world recession ensues. Then the need to fight unemployment might also come into prominence in the North American continent and even in the world's leading economy, the United States.

In order to provide a theoretical justification for this suggested way of development, let us start from Krugman's (1994:30-32) analysis "in a highly simplified nutshell" of "the Keynesian theory of recession and recovery", which, as Krugman (ibid., p. 32) says, "remains one of the great achievements of economic thought". I will try to sum up a part of Krugman's apt analysis even more concisely, if possible. As he says (ibid., p. 31), "the usual and basic Keynesian answer to recessions is a monetary expansion". As Keynes (1936:234) himself writes when tackling the possibilities of decreasing "the money-rate of interest": "The only relief...can come (so long as the propensity towards liquidity is unchanged) from an increase in the quantity of money, or - which is formally the same thing - a rise in the value of money which enables a given quantity to provide increased money-services". When analysing the "wage- and price-level" (ibid., pp. 266-268) Keynes also points out: "A change in the quantity of money...is already within the power of most governments by open-market policy or analogous measures. Having regard to human nature and our institutions, it can only be a foolish person who would prefer a flexible wage policy to a flexible money policy...Moreover, other things being equal, a method which it is comparatively easy to apply should be deemed preferable to a method which is probably so difficult as to be impracticable" (ibid., pp. 267-268).

Krugman (1994:32) characterizes a second main point in Keynes's ideas as follows: "The Keynesian answer to a liquidity trap is for the government to do what the private sector will not: spend. When monetary expansion is ineffective, fiscal expansion - such as public works programs financed by borrowing - must take its place."

In the chapter "Notes on the Trade Cycle" Keynes (1936:313-332) himself analyses the dynamics of the "cyclical fluctuation" (ibid., p. 319) and he also raises some other ideas as possible remedies. He proposes, for instance, "to promote investment and, at the same time, to promote consumption, not merely to the level which with the existing propensity to consume would correspond to the increased investment, but to a higher level still" (ibid., p. 325). He says that "whilst aiming at a socially controlled rate of investment...I should support at the same time all sorts of policies for increasing the propensity to consume" (ibid.).

Nevertheless, historically and also in our present world Krugman (1994:32) is perfectly right when he points to Keynes's idea of "public works programs" (ibid.) as the second main Keynesian remedy. Keynes (1936:320) himself emphasizes that "in conditions of laissez-faire the avoidance of wide fluctuations in employment may, therefore, prove impossible without a far-reaching change in the psychology of investment markets such as there is no reason to expect. I conclude that the duty of ordering the current volume of investment cannot safely be left in private hands".

Within the chapter of "Concluding Notes on the Social Philosophy towards which the General Theory might lead" Keynes (1936:377-378) emphasizes "the vital importance of establishing certain central controls in matters which are now left in the main to individual initiative...". He continues: "The State will have to exercise a guiding influence on the propensity to consume partly through its scheme of taxation, partly by fixing the rate of interest, and partly, perhaps, in other ways. Furthermore, it seems unlikely that the influence on banking policy on the rate of interest will be sufficient by itself to determine an optimum rate of investment. I conceive, therefore, that a somewhat comprehensive socialisation of investment will prove the only means of securing an approximation to full employment; though this need not exclude all manner of compromises and of devices by which public authority will co-operate with private initiative." This is in fact a brilliant description of what we can call today a mixed economy.

In some other sentences of this important paragraph Keynes (ibid., p. 378) carefully demarcates this vision from what he calls "a system of State Socialism which would embrace most of the economic life of the community". As he says: "It is not the ownership of the instruments of production which it is important for the State to assume. If the State is able to determine the aggregate amount of resources devoted to augmenting the instruments and the basic rate of reward to those who own them, it will have accomplished all that is necessary."

Keynes's ideas about public works programs are timely even today, around the turn of the millenium. As regards contemporary suggestions about public investments in education, research, as well as infrastructure, see, for instance, Edin (1995a:15-16). But in our days the public sector could and should go half a step further than most of the conventional Keynesian expansionist measures. In addition to helping the economy by government orders, total output can also be grown through increasing the size of the public sector itself by employing more people in welfare services. In this case the employers are various organizations belonging to the public sector, frequently education and health care institutions under the control of county councils and municipal offices. This would solve the problem expressed, for instance, by Stephens (1996:58), when he worried that "it is not at all clear what sectors would produce the new jobs. Job growth in Scandinavia has been almost entirely a product of the expansion of public services in the past two decades and it is widely agreed that this pattern cannot continue. Manufacturing is not producing significant increases in employment in relative terms in any of the advanced industrial economies."

The facts revealed by Stephens (ibid.) are correct and very significant, but the remark that "it is widely agreed that this pattern cannot continue" is inaccurate. Widely agreed by whom? Either by conservatively oriented social scientists or some of their progressive colleagues who got into a pessimistic mood because in a yielding moment they had fallen for an erroneous conservative argument. The point is precisely that the "pattern" aptly described by Stephens, namely "the expansion of public services" as "almost entirely" the source of "job growth" still can and indeed should continue in many of "the advanced industrial economies". What Esping-Andersen (1999:15) described as "the massive employment-generating effect of welfare state expansion in education, health, and social services", which "occurred ... from the mid-1960s onward", can continue, even if perhaps on a somewhat more modest scale, but supported by deliberately giving the public sector the financial means to be the direct employer of the welfare service employees, and switching off market mediation in this process of enlargement.

In this case the pessimistic scenario sketched by Esping-Andersen (ibid., pp. 13-14) that "if we desire full employment, we must scale back social citizenship and job rights. If we wish to restore full employment, we may have to accept levels of inequality that neither pluralist theory nor welfare state ideology would have found acceptable.", in other words, "the great 'equality-or-jobs' trade-off", or the "new conflict between equality and employment" (Esping-Andersen 1996a:4), is not unavoidable.

He writes about the solution elsewhere when he first describes that "(i)n a service-led economy (the) cost-disease translates easily into jobless growth"(Esping-Andersen 1999:112). Then he reveals that "there is, of course, a ... possible solution, namely to subsidize services - either directly via government production, or indirectly via subsidies to consumers. All advanced nations have to a greater or lesser degree adopted the subsidy strategy, especially for vital collective goods such as health and education ... The European nations stress direct public provision, the United States favours tax-subsidized private provision. The uniqueness of Scandinavia lies in government's huge role in furnishing labour-intensive, and otherwise unaffordable, care services to families. Hence, Scandinavian tertiarization is uniquely biased towards welfare state jobs and away from market services." (ibid., pp. 112-113). This latter is precisely the solution which can invariably also provide a cure for unemployment, we can add.

Esping-Andersen's (ibid., p. 113) conclusion is that "(t)he limits of subsidization are a question of political economy: of the balance of political power and citizens' willingness to be taxed". It is evident that our suggested solution is a widely existing practice, except for the mentioned tax-financing, the Achilles' heel of the matter.

Naturally, when we suggest that the public sector can and should again provide a cure for unemployment today and tomorrow, as opposed to the recently highly fashionable magic of the "market", we have entered the rather delicate spheres of contemporary social science controversy. This question, together with the "discretionism versus rulism" and the "unemployment versus inflation as the main problem" debates (cf. Johansson 1994a:269 about the Maastricht Treaty), as well as the "labour market deregulation" question, belongs to the very heart of the general political and ideological confrontation between progressive and conservative trends within the modern Western world in our age.

As regards the "Swedish model" of the welfare state, Ahrne (1994a:39) is certainly right when he says that solidarity which is attributed to the welfare state is strongly limited. In spite of this, it is too early to speak of the Swedish model and the welfare state in the past tense as Ahrne and (Roine) Johansson (1994:115) and Ahrne (1995:63) regrettably do. The ostensible decline of the Swedish model from the early 1990s onwards was the sad result of wrong governmental economic policies, a number of serious mistakes. This has been thoroughly analysed and revealed by Sten Johansson (1994a:262-263, 270, 278 Notes 12. and 15.; 1997 and 1998), Ekdahl (1999 about Sten Johansson), Edin and Andersson (1995:2-3, 6, 13-18), as well as Korpi (1990, 1992, 1996a and 1996b, pp. 132-133 in particular), and Benner (1997:221-222, 1998:141-142).

The welfare state in general and the Swedish model in particular are alive and they will probably have a much greater future than many social scientists dare to believe today.

COMBINED KEYNESIAN EXPANSION

The basic idea on which some elements of a modern mixed economy can be built may originate in a combination of what Krugman (1994:32) aptly summarized as the two main historical methods emerging from Keynes's ideas. In other words, a proper combination of "monetary expansion" with "public works programs" (ibid.) can be useful to cure sluggish growth, recession and high unemployment in our modern Western society. This means that "public works programs" should no longer be "financed by borrowing", but could be financed by an appropriate measure of simultaneous "monetary expansion" (ibid.). Saying 'appropriate measure' involves an understanding that the whole exercise will not lead to any significant degree to increased inflation.

As regards the first method, monetary expansion alone, it is allegedly not usable to raise output and decrease unemployment in a market economy. Whether in the long run, according to Friedman (1968), or already in the short run if it can be anticipated, and it always can be, according to Lucas (see 1972, 1995), a governmentally induced monetary expansion, the first Keynesian curing method in Krugman's (1994:32) description, is still supposed by dominant circles of economists today not to have lasting real effects.

As regards the second historical Keynesian method of curing recessions with "public works programs financed by borrowing" (Krugman 1994:32), it is criticized for causing the "crowding out" of private expansion by taking away the capital from private investments and thus being ineffective in raising the overall level of employment in a country (cf. Friedman 1973: point 9, Gill 1976:123, Dornbusch and Fischer 1990:149-155). So, both of the main historical methods offered by Keynesian theory to cure recessions, according to Krugman (1994:32), are still criticized to a considerable extent by contemporary economics.

But again: why not combine these two main methods? As mentioned, the idea is to initiate "public works programs", or as Keynes (1936:378) himself put it, "a somewhat comprehensive socialisation of investment", however, financed not by "borrowing", but by an appropriate size of monetary expansion.

To make our idea more precise: the "public works programs" should not be arbitrarily contrived plans of superfluous works. In this respect Joan Robinson's (1973a:10) suggestion to "(d)ig holes in the ground and fill them again, paint the Black Forest white; if men cannot be paid wages for doing something sensible, pay them to do something silly" is in fact not a good idea. Fortunately, Robinson (ibid.) immediately quotes her master, Keynes (1936:220) about this: "'To dig holes in the ground', paid for out of savings, will increase, not only employment but the real national dividend of useful goods and services. It is not reasonable, however," Keynes adds "that a sensible community should be content to remain dependent on such fortuitous and often wasteful mitigations when once we understand the influences upon which effective demand depends."

Indeed, there are many reasonable tasks in society to be performed. Besides improving the infrastructure of a country, first and foremost the quantity and quality of the welfare services, or "personal services" in the denotation of Halmos (1970), should be improved by employing additional labour force within the public sector. In Sweden a somewhat similar suggestion has already been put forward by Professor Bo Rothstein (1996).

The advantages of such a combined method of curing slumps can be twofold. Let us reverse the order and take first the problem of "crowding out" of private investment. If public sector growth is financed not by tax increases or by selling new bonds to the public, but by monetization, that is to say, creating new money in the central bank and giving it to the government, in exchange for either bonds or even a piece of paper promising gradual repayment in 50 years, then there is no crowding out of private investment and no contraction in the private sector at all. Then there is an actual monetary expansion; the cake of the money growth is not merely redistributed between the private and the public sectors, but its aggregate size is increased to finance the increased growth of the latter.

Of course, this flies in the face of all shades of the currently prevailing dogmas of conservative economics, above all the monetarist and the rational expectations schools. Within the European Union this also flies in the face of the Maastricht Treaty, even those paragraphs regulating the second stage of the Economic and Monetary Union (EMU), let alone those regulating the third stage, the actual way of introducing the planned common currency, the Euro. Thus some significant changes would be necessary here (cf., for instance, Johansson and Wibe 1998 about the misconceived independence of the central banks).

The other advantage on the theoretical level of the suggested Keynesian combination of monetary expansion and public works programs concerns the arguments often summed up under the concept of the "neutrality of money". It concerns both the already widely accepted long-run version of Friedman (1968), together with Phelps's (1967 and 1968) arguments refuting would-be solutions based on the Phillips curve, and the more extreme short-term version of Lucas and his disciples. As we have seen, Lucas's standpoint has already been questioned and refuted by prominent Keynesian economists, but in spite of that, sadly enough, it is still prevalent in many places of political and economic power.

But not even Friedman's and Phelps's milder and generally accepted arguments concerning the long run are valid if the employer is directly a part of the public sector (and, of course, the managers of the employer's activities are not the followers of conservative macroeconomics). Then the effects of a monetary expansion on employment cannot be questioned with the help of the gradual, adaptive price-adjustment process revealed by Friedman and Phelps, because the employment effects of a monetary expansion take place directly, that is, mostly outside and without the wheeling and dealing of the market economy analysed by Friedman and Phelps. If a monetary expansion is not simply pumped into the usual veins of the market economy, for instance, by open market purchase of bonds by the central bank from the commercial banks, that is, increasing bank reserves and the monetary base, but the new money is given specifically to the public sector to be the direct employer, then the arguments about the neutrality of money may be invalid even in the long run.

Neither in this case will the public sector commission goods or services from private firms in the way the story of a traditional Keynesian fiscal expansion has been told up to now; instead, the public sector now becomes the employer of the newly employed labour force directly. There both main participants in the economic game, the employees and the employers, will behave differently from what is characteristic of the private sector in a typical market economy, described by Friedman (1968) and Phelps (1967, 1968).

According to Robinson (1973a:7), "(t)he level of money wages in any country at any time is more or less an historical accident going back to a remote past and influenced by recent events affecting the balance of power between employers and trade unions in the labour market". The significance of such a balance of power in both economic and political resources, for welfare in general and also for unemployment as well as wage formation in the labour market, is emphasized in particular by Walter Korpi (1978, 1982, 1983, 1987a, 1987b and 1991). It is precisely this originally more or less conflictory character of the labour market relations which may be mitigated considerably and turned into co-operation within the public sector in the future.

Then wages might still be formally negotiated in more or less the same way as earlier, in Europe mainly with the trade unions. However, the trade unions of public employees may well look at their public sector employers more favourably if many new jobs are created. They may well behave considerably more mildly, influenced by political sympathy, and in fact their wages, salaries may be set in a different way from what was supposed by Friedman and Phelps.

Even more significant differences lie hidden in the behaviour of the employers, who are in practice various officials within the public sector. (Of course, we suppose that they do not follow any doctrines of the prevailing conservative economics, either the monetarist or the rational expectations version.) The employers within the public sector will then neither raise the prices of the welfare services nor decrease employment, neither in the short run nor in the long run. Then the necessary money is simply provided by means of a monetary expansion, because the public sector as the employer is not led by business considerations, that is to say, by the principle of profit maximization. Then the public sector may well be guided by ethical considerations, or if you like, by political considerations, behind which there have to be moral considerations and social interests in a genuinely democratic society.

For the bulk of the public sector the "economic conflict grounded in price-setting struggles", according to Ingham (1998:1), is then for the most part over. Ingham (ibid., p. 13) also says, after Weber, that money's "purchasing power can only be established through the struggle between producers and possessors of both money and goods", and he quotes Weber's (1978:108) assertion that "(p)rices are expressions of the struggle; they are instruments of calculation only as estimated quantifications of relative chances in this struggle of interests". But for the bulk of the public sector of the economy such struggles can by and large be avoided in the future.

To put it in another way: if and when the public sector is the employer in the welfare services, then the functioning of these services may to a considerable degree be removed from the framework of the market economy, from the conditions of the market. Then the profit principle may become irrelevant in those services, and the "neutrality of money" types of argument, by either Friedman or Phelps, tied inseparably to the market economy, automatically lose their validity. Then a monetary expansion will directly lead to new public employment, both in the short run and the long run. The combined expansion under discussion gives all the new money to the public sector, and this ensures that every penny is used to increase output and not prices. On the other hand, the monetization of the necessary expenses by the central bank ensures that there is no increase in the budget deficit. The suggested method of combined expansion can be perceived as consisting of the present market economy as it is today plus one big self-financing public economic entity added to it.

A process of curing a recession with the suggested combined Keynesian expansion thus cannot be subject to the effects of the market economy described by Friedman (1968) and Phelps (1967, 1968), and consequently it will ensure a lasting solution, one which does not disappear in the long run.

Of course, adding a sizable self-financing public "enterprise" to the market economy does not at all mean that the public and the private sectors are isolated from each other. Therefore the level of aggregate demand and aggregate supply in the economy as a whole will increase, and Keynes's (1936:113-131) multiplier may forecast how much these parameters of the whole economy will increase. Such increases may then be considerably larger than those amounts corresponding merely to the size of the initiating increment in direct employment within the public sector.

But what about the gradual, adaptive upward price-adjustment processes working in the "long run", revealed by Friedman (1968) and Phelps (1967, 1968)? Well, yes, much later, in the "long run", a certain small part of the multiplied increase in output may gradually be eroded by the adaptive price-rise phenomena within the private sector of the economy. So what? Anything resembling a complete return to the original state of affairs that prevailed before the initial increase in public sector direct employment under discussion is out of the question, and so is the illusion of the "neutrality of money" concerning the whole process. The amount of money created and used in tangible, direct employment growth within the public sector is far from being neutral. And in addition it generates a multiplied increase in output within the whole economy.

To sum up, again briefly, the main theoretical elements in the suggested method of combined Keynesian expansion (CKE), the following components may be mentioned:

1./ The Keynesian "public works programs" idea.

2./ A simultaneous monetary expansion to finance them.

3./ The new jobs should come mainly in welfare services.

4./ The new jobs should come as direct public sector employment.

The simultaneous application of the ideas under points 1. and 2. actually means a combination of fiscal policy and monetary policy. According to Hillier (1991:53), such a combination can be considered via "a money-financed increase in government spending". He also refers to Tinbergen's (1952) "more general result" that "in order to achieve a number of targets simultaneously, it is necessary to have at least as many independent instruments or tools as there are targets" (citation from Hillier 1991:55), when he shows that "by a judicious combination of policies the government can achieve not only a target level of income, but, simultaneously, a target rate of interest which it may desire to achieve in order to encourage private investment" (ibid., p. 54). Hillier (ibid., pp.53-55, Figures 2.8 and 2.9) also illustrates the "joint use of fiscal and monetary policies" in figures, showing that in the IS-LM model both the IS and the LM curves were moved to the right when such a combined fiscal and monetary expansion is applied by a government. As a result, output is always increased, while the value of the interest rate can be regulated conveniently: it can remain unchanged, or either increase or decrease, if necessary.

As regards other kinds of graphic illustrations, for example, the aggregate supply and aggregate demand curves, sometimes abbreviated as the "AS-AD model" (cf., for instance, Hillier ibid., p. 143 ff), it is easy to understand that as a result of a combined expansion, output, measured along the horizontal axis, is increased for both the supply and the demand curves representing the original market economy conditions before a governmental action, and thus after a combined expansion both the supply and the demand curves will shift to the right. This also stands for the 'full employment' output, represented by a vertical line, in fact an asymptote if it is the theoretical maximum, which also shifts to the right. Such shifts will ensue both in the original, "static" versions of the AS-AD curves, where the price level is on the vertical axis, and in the "dynamic" versions, where inflation is on the vertical axis. The answer to a question as to what extent the price level or the rate of inflation on the vertical axis is increased after a combined expansion may depend on various factors, and some of these may be dealt with later on.

The directives under points 3. and 4. above represent, so to say, the practical implementations of the combination of fiscal and monetary policies embodied in the principles under points 1. and 2. At the same time CKE as a whole represents a kind of synthesis between activist, that is, discretionist policies influencing the aggregate demand side and those influencing the aggregate supply side of the economy, it is to some extent a combination of both (cf., for instance, Dornbusch, Fischer and Startz 1998:174-177 about theoretical debates on the problem of priority belonging to aggregate demand fluctuations versus aggregate supply fluctuations).

There may be some questions about the suggested method of combined expansion, and those that come to mind first are perhaps the following: what about efficiency, what about the size of needed monetary expansions under discussion, and what about inflation?

As regards efficiency, the brief answer is that in the welfare or, with Halmos's (1970) term, personal services this is not the main requirement, not the main criterion of functioning properly. The main criteria in these services have to be ethical, based on the quality of human life and the wellbeing of the recipients. Naturally, however, this is not an excuse for squandering resources. Reasonable limits of spending already exist in the contemporary practice of welfare services, with corresponding functioning systems of supervision and control. There is no need to apply additional financial incentives, namely the cruel principles of the market economy, based on the goal of profit maximization, in the public welfare services. As the earlier mentioned saying about a corn-cutting turned into amputation illustrates, a drive for efficiency and achievement based on the profit principle may in this sphere become counterproductive, even dangerous.

The questions about the size of necessary monetary expansions in general and of the possible inflationary effects will be dealt with in later chapters.

NONINFLATIONARY MONETIZATION REVISITED

These chapters or at least a considerable part of them can be considered as a kind of supplement to Sollenius (1996). But there is a significant difference: now the term noninflationary monetization will be used in a wider sense, in order to include several versions or methods of monetization, that is to say, creation of money by the central bank to support the public sector, which can avoid having inflationary consequences. We can now mention the following versions:

1./ The method called "direct monetization" with "direct government spending" (ibid., p.43).

2./ Monetization of the interest burden on the external debt without increasing domestic inflation.

3./ Free of expense bond-financing of the consolidated public sector debt, with a different way of accounting for the effective national debt.

"DIRECT MONETIZATION"

After conversations with a few prominent economists I now consider it necessary to make a somewhat more detailed proposal about possible financial techniques of a method mentioned earlier. (In particular, I am greatly indebted to Professor Franco Modigliani in the United States and to Professor Börje Kragh in Sweden for valuable remarks and suggestions, and also to Professors James Tobin and Rudi Dornbusch in the United States for comments and advice in shorter telephone conversations.) These techniques primarily concern what I called "direct monetization" and "direct government spending" in Figure 2 on page 43 of Sollenius (1996). Naturally, there are various financial techniques that can be used to implement the ideas proposed. So what I present below may comprise only a few of numerous possible suggestions.

Let us see, for example, how the interest burden of 100 million Crowns on maturing old debt can be paid with money created "with a stroke of the pen". In the T-accounts below A stands for assets and L for liabilities. Only the changes relevant for the explanation are indicated.

Step One

Central bank (Fed)	
A	L
Government bonds or a bill of debt + 100	Treasury deposit + 100

The central bank buys 100 million Crowns worth of government securities direct from the treasury, without involving any commercial bank or any kind of dealer. Or, in another case, for example, the treasury issues a letter promising to pay back 100 million Crowns in 50 years, received as a non-interest loan direct from the central bank. In practice there is not much difference between these two cases, because "at the end of the year" the central bank "turns over most of its interest earnings to the treasury anyway" (Ritter and Silber 1983:262). The money appears on the account of the treasury at the central bank.

Step Two

Central bank (Fed)		Treasury	
A	L	A	L
	Treasury deposit − 100	"Letter of transfer" + 100	Debt to central bank + 100
	"Treasury liability" + 100		

In Step Two the central bank sends a specific, newly-introduced "letter of transfer" to the treasury, providing it with the right to hold and distribute the amount of 100 million Crowns. No money is moved in physical form. The treasury's deposit at the central bank is reduced by 100 million Crowns; instead, the amount appears on a newly-created, indicative account as outstanding "treasury liability".

Step Three

Commercial banks	
A	L
"Treasury transfers" + 90	Treasury deposits + 100
Remitted reserves + 10	

The treasury distributes 90 million Crowns to its "tax and loan accounts" at those banks commissioned with selling government bonds and also with redeeming their interest-bearing coupons. The treasury does so by sending out specific, newly-introduced "treasury transfers" to, say, 50 big commercial bank offices directly, avoiding the use of the general bank clearing system and thereby the reserve deposits of the commercial banks held at the central bank. In this way no high-powered money but only face-value money is released. This is an essential point of the method.

The newly-introduced "treasury transfers", henceforth TTs, which the banks are obliged to accept, have some specific characteristics in order to ensure the above condition, namely the face-value feature of the released money. Their most important characteristic is that the money they carry is not allowed to be used to increase bank reserves.

No part of their amounts is allowed to be put on the reserve accounts of the commercial banks held at the central bank. Hence they cannot become excess reserves for the banks and thus cannot become the source of a deposit expansion process by the banking system. This is what is meant by saying that they cannot function as high-powered money, only as face-value money.

Because of this ban on using any part of the money carried by the TTs as reserves, the treasury also remits appropriate amounts of reserves to all the commercial banks in question. These amounts are calculated so that, according to the rules of fractional reserve banking, they are enough to support the money needed for the interest payments when it temporarily appears in the form of new deposits on the accounts of the treasury held at these "distributing" banks. (For the sake of simplicity we now suppose that the reciprocal of the money multiplier can by and large be regarded as a kind of aggregate reserve rate for the whole banking system. Considering the M2 money aggregate, let us suppose that its money multiplier is now exactly 10.) The remittance of reserves is made in order to save these banks from getting into a disadvantageous financial position as regards reserves when they receive the money intended for interest payments.

While the TTs - whether in written or electronic form - are sent in ways avoiding the reserve accounts of the commercial banks held at the central bank, the accompanying reserves can be remitted by the treasury through the general bank-clearing system, usually functioning under the direction of the central bank. This system may forward remittances in any form when it is initiated by the treasury; in our example the 10 million reserves may start as a part of the earlier 100 million received by the treasury from the central bank. This 10 million remittance sent back will then reduce outstanding "treasury liability" to 90 million, as we shall see later. The result of this phase is that 90 million Crowns of TTs and 10 million Crowns of remitted reserves are received by the "distributing" commercial banks, and the total amount of 100 million appears on the deposits of the treasury held at these banks.

Step Four

Commercial banks	
A	L
TTs at distributing banks - 90	Treasury deposits - 100
TTs at other banks + 90	Deposits of nonbank public + 100
Reserves of distr. banks - 10	
Reserves of other banks + 10	

In paying the interest burden on bonds (or paying back the principal sums as well) the distributing banks forward the money from the accounts of the treasury they hold to the bank accounts of the individual holders of the bonds in question in the same way as they received it. (In the example all bond-holders are supposed to have their accounts at other banks.) In other words, they divide the money up according to the individual payments, regroup them according to the receiving banks, and then forward the total of 90 million Crowns by means of new, smaller value "treasury transfers" released by them and addressed to the other banks. At the same time they also remit the divided and regrouped parts of the 10 million Crowns of accompanying bank reserves to the receiving banks through the general bank-clearing system.

Paying the interest burden on the public debt is described now as a two-phased process only because the treasury (or its branch offices) usually has no capacity to send payments directly to the large number of individual bond-holders. If the treasury had enough capacity to perform all the individual transactions there would be no need to rely on the mediating role of the "distributing banks".

Step One is not a common practice today, but it would be easy to carry out within the present framework of financial institutions, apart from the precondition within the EU that the prohibition of direct monetization imposed in the Maastricht Treaty must first be abolished. As regards the introduction of the "letter of transfer" and the "treasury transfers" mentioned in Steps Two, Three and Four, which can be implemented through any kinds of documented means of telecommunication, as well as written transactions, these techniques are indeed new, but in fact they require only minor legislative, administrative changes, easy to carry out and well worth the effort.

Returning to our example, at the end of the four steps the government has paid some of its interest burden on a stock of debt (or has paid back the principal sums too in case of maturing old debt) to the extent of 100 million Crowns and the nonbank public have received this amount on their bank deposits. (The bonds are not shown in our T-accounts, only the coupons are indicated.) The relevant changes after this process of "direct monetization" and "direct spending" are shown below.

Central bank		Commercial banks		Nonbank public	
A	L	A	L	A	L
Government bonds +100	"Treasury liability" +90				
	Bank reserves +10	Bank reserves +10			
		"Treasury transfers" +90	Deposits of nonbank public +100	Deposits in commercial banks +100	
				Coupons of old bonds −100	

In exchange for bonds printed by the treasury or for a bill of debt, the central bank created money "with a stroke of the pen", and with this money the government paid the interest on old debt (or paid back the principal sums) without allowing the release of significant amounts of high-powered money during the process. The great bulk of the 100 million Crowns released is only face-value money; this is ensured by the specific characteristics of the new kind of assets called "treasury transfers". They are not allowed to be put on the accounts at the central bank that hold the reserves of the commercial banks, thus they cannot become excess reserves. Nor are they allowed to be lent out to other banks as parts of loans in any other form. These rules serve the purpose of preventing the usual "chain-lending", the deposit-expansion process by the banking system. In other words, these rules serve the purpose of preserving the face-value money quality of the TTs, as opposed to the high-powered money on the reserve accounts of the commercial banks.

What on earth, then, can the commercial banks do with the TTs? They can just keep them. They are the assets standing behind the new deposits of the nonbank public, received as interest and principal payments on maturing government bonds. However, the commercial banks have an obligation to pay interest to the nonbank public on the new deposits in the future, at least on those which are left with them and not consumed or invested elsewhere. Are the TTs as assets not capable of earning revenue for the banks in order to pay for the future obligation to pay interest?

In order not to put the commercial banks in an unfavourable financial situation, the TTs should be given at least one and possibly two further points of advantage, in addition to being accompanied by remitted reserves, as mentioned above. Namely, the treasury should pay the commercial banks interest on all TTs held by them permanently (that is, in the case of the "distributing banks" mentioned: on all TTs received minus those forwarded to other banks). Since it is impossible to follow the future lots of the great many individual payments made by means of TTs, concerning the ways the receiving bank clients use them, whether they spend them or on what kinds of accounts and how long they keep them, the treasury pays an average interest rate on the TTs to the commercial banks for a year or two. This rate of interest is recommended to be considerably lower than the yield of new government bonds, because the method under discussion is intended to be monetization, that is, money financing of the public debt, as opposed to bond financing.

The second further point of advantage attached to the TTs is the possibility that after a number of years, say, five or ten years, the commercial banks may be allowed to buy government bonds for the accumulated TTs they hold, provided the conditions of the outstanding stock of public debt in the country allow this. Such purchases cannot be allowed immediately, because that would bring the whole process back to the bad old situation of debt financing, that is, bond financing. After a number of years of economic recovery, however, the public debt situation in the country will probably improve, and this may make such bond purchases possible. The government may even allow some commercial banks selectively to do so, and the extent of taking into consideration the inflation in the years passed when fixing the price of the purchased bonds may also be determined selectively.

With accompanying bank reserves remitted and interest paid on the TTs the method under discussion will probably succeed in leaving the finances of the commercial banks in balance, not imposing any specific burden on them, at least not before a possible anti-inflationary, counterbalancing action is started by the central bank, which we will discuss below. But even if this method of stabilizing public finances were to impose some measure of temporary burden on the banking system, judged from a historical point of view such an event should not be considered unfair at all. From the early 1980s onwards a process of deregulation has been evolving in the advanced industrial societies concerning all kinds of financial activities and the banking sector of the economy. This is an essential part of an emerging neoconservative wave in both economic theory and socio-economic practice during the latest two and a half decades. Borrowing Ehrenberg's (1995:passim and pp. 94, 113, in particular) expression, one can observe that a systemic change ("systemskiftet") is taking place in the advanced Western world which allows an unprecedented boom for finance and banking, above all for speculative financial activities (cf. ibid., pp. 26, 30) and at the same time it imposes restrictions and heavy curtailments on the welfare institutions of society. The welfare system is cut back rigorously, while the financial institutions have never had it so good as today. Hence it would be completely justified if some contingent burdens of stabilizing government finances had to be endured by the rich, blossoming financial sector and not by the restricted or destroyed welfare institutions and the people they take care of, that is, by the young, the old, the sick, the poor.

However, the bankers themselves may consider our method to be one withholding some of their theoretical profits. When the treasury pays for the interest burden on the public debt with TTs it keeps the commercial banks in a more or less unchanged, balanced financial situation, but if it let the TTs be exchanged for highly profitable government bonds immediately, that would serve their profits much better. Their relative dissatisfaction might induce the banks to raise their interest rates on loans in order to compensate themselves for the lost profits that could have been obtained in theory from new bonds, had the traditional bond financing system of the public debt been continued. A desire for compensation on the part of the banks may also arise if previously eliminated reserve requirements (as in the Swedish practice in the spring of 1994) are reintroduced for the sake of the method, or if the interest paid by the treasury on the TTs is considered too low or too short-termed, and finally if the bourgeois press whips up all the bankers' dissatisfaction.

The central bank, which - we now suppose - co-operates with the government closely, is able to influence short-term market interest rates to some extent by changing its discount rate and its repurchase agreement ("repo") interest rates. Hence it can eliminate or decrease the effects of possible raising of interest rates by the commercial banks. Nevertheless, it is prudent, if - as an indirect consequence of the raising of interest rates on loans by the commercial banks - we reckon with a measure of rise in the average interest rate on the outstanding stock of public debt, as described in the equations below.

Let us start with the key formula for the growth of the stock of public debt, in the version explicated in more detail on p. 18 of Sollenius (1996), following Dornbusch and Fischer (1990:614, 628), and examine the state of affairs when the change in b, that is, the change in the debt per GNP ratio, is zero. This means that the ratio of the outstanding public debt to GNP does not grow any further; in other words, the public debt is stabilized:

The change of $b = b(r-y) - x = b(i-p-y) - x = 0$

Here r is the real interest rate, i is the nominal interest rate, p is the rate of inflation, y is the real growth rate and x is the noninterest or primary surplus measured as a fraction of GNP. From this we conclude that the critical, stabilizing value of the nominal interest rate is:

$i_o = x/b + y + p$.

As a result of the process of monetization, we can reckon with a new, theoretical, "monetized" interest rate concerning the interest burden on the outstanding public debt:

$$i_m = c \cdot i(1-q) + j \cdot q .$$

Here c is a factor of increase in the average nominal interest rate on the public debt that might come into being indirectly because the commercial banks might increase their interest rates on loans, in order to compensate for some theoretically lost profits they believe in. The value of c is a little over 1. Then q is the ratio of the monetized part of the yearly interest burden to the whole amount of the yearly interest burden on the public debt. The value of q is between 0 and 1. Finally, j is the nominal interest rate paid on the TTs.

In the critical, stabilizing case $i_m = i_o$. From this we conclude that:

$$q = (c \cdot i - i_o) / (c \cdot i - j)$$

or if we denote $c \cdot i = i_r$, the nominal interest rate possibly raised by the actions of the banks, we can write:

$$q = (i_r - i_o) / (i_r - j) .$$

Here q gives the minimum portion of the yearly interest burden of the public debt needed to be monetized with our method in order to accomplish the stabilized state of the outstanding public debt as regards its ratio to GNP. One can see that the lower c and i, the higher i_o, that is to say, the higher x, y, p and the lower b, furthermore the lower j, the smaller q is needed. From this it is obvious that in practice the choice of q can be strongly influenced by the general goals of economic policy in the country in question.

"In a Keynesian mode", to borrow an expression from Tobin (1987, sub-title), with priority given to fighting high unemployment before the goal of decreasing inflation to zero, it is natural to choose the value of each of the above-mentioned parameters, if possible, in a way favourable to stabilizing the outstanding stock of public debt. That is, the central bank should decrease or keep its discount rate and 'repo' interest rates at comparatively low levels, which will influence market interest rates and can decrease c and i. At the same time such a policy can stimulate the whole economy, and as a consequence, both y, the real growth rate and x, the primary surplus will increase.

If in the meantime p, the inflation rate, also increases moderately, in a Keynesian framework this should not be considered a tragedy. From the viewpoint of stabilizing the stock of public debt, inflation is in theory definitely preferable, as is well-known. Of course, this must not allow a policy of letting inflation break loose, but the priorities of economic policy as regards a choice between inflation and unemployment in society should be determined in a more balanced way. My view is that 5 percent inflation with 5 percent unemployment is better than zero inflation with 10 percent unemployment.

Returning to our example, we notice that had the money been spent in the traditional way of monetization, that is, paid into the reserve accounts of the commercial banks held at the central bank, then high-powered money amounting to 100 million Crowns would have been released. The banks would have added this money to their reserve deposits as excess reserves. Then by means of "chain-lending", that is, the usual process of deposit expansion by the banking system, the deposits of the public would finally have grown by the money multiplier times, that is, in our case, 10 times the released amount of high-powered money: by 1000 million Crowns. That would have caused a somewhat more significant increase in the money supply.

The 100 million Crowns deposit increase in the hands of the nonbank public in our example is a much more modest increase in the money supply, but it still represents a certain degree of increase, and in theory it could still lead to some expansionary and hence inflationary consequences, unless it is counterbalanced. Before looking at the necessity as such to counterbalance it or not, let us first see how it can be counterbalanced by an open market sale of 10 million Crowns worth of government bonds by the central bank, if necessary.

Here that very favourable attribute of fractional reserve banking is used which makes it possible to control much greater amounts of face-value money by clever leverage of comparatively small amounts of money - the bank reserves - which are, however, placed in a key position. As mentioned in Sollenius (1996:49-52) but is also well-known, an "m" times smaller amount of bonds is to be sold. The changes resulting from such a typical open market sale will be shown below. These changes take place after a time lag needed for the impact of the open market operation to work its way through the banking system (cf., for instance, Dornbusch and Fischer 1990:448 and 456-457, as well as Ritter and Silber 1983:450-451).

Central bank		Commercial banks		Nonbank public	
A	L	A	L	A	L
Bonds - 10				Bonds + 10	
		Bank reserves - 10	Bank reserves - 10		
		New loans - 90			New loans - 90
			New deposits - 100	New deposits - 100	

As we saw, the reserves of the commercial banks had previously been increased by 10 million Crowns via remittances from the treasury in order to hold enough reserves against the 100 million Crowns of new deposits received by means of the TTs. It is precisely this increase in bank reserves which is to be counterbalanced, if necessary, by the subsequent open market sale of 10 million Crowns worth of bonds (to the public in our example). As we now see, the consequent 10 million Crowns decrease in bank reserves leads to a 10 times larger decrease in the money supply in the next round of lending, in the next round of deposit creation by the commercial banks, given that the money multiplier is exactly 10.

If the central bank draws in reserves from the banking system by means of open market sales for the purpose of counterbalancing the rise in the money supply represented by the new deposits, then this may well leave the banking system with inadequate reserves. Then the commercial banks may borrow reserves from the central bank, they may borrow reserves from each other, and they may also choose to sell some of their assets, probably some government bonds, either to other banks or to the nonbank public, in order to obtain reserves. Whether the banks choose the alternative of selling bonds and what the extent of such a sale would be depend on various factors, mainly on the comparative values of the discount rate, i.e. the price of borrowing from the central bank, the inter-bank borrowing rate ("federal funds rate" in the United States), and the market interest rates on various kinds of bonds. These questions may also depend on other factors, e.g. the speed and portioning or schedule of the financial processes under discussion, the general economic situation in the country, the specific financial conditions of the individual banks, etc. If the banks choose to sell bonds to each other in order to obtain reserves, then this may take the shape of a classic process of deposit contraction within the banking system (cf. Ritter and Silber 1983:49-51), and the final result of such a process may be the purchase of the bonds in question by the nonbank public.

However, such a process should not be mistaken for the selling of bonds to the nonbank public by the treasury, because it is far from being equivalent to it. In the latter case brand new bonds would be sold to the public by the treasury, with a brand new interest burden on them. That would be simple debt-financing of the budget deficit. In contrast, our example may only involve the possible redistribution of some already outstanding old bonds, which might change hands between the commercial banks and the public; from the viewpoint of the accumulated public debt and the budget deficit this is meaningless. In our example, which is a case of money-financing of the budget deficit, only 10 million Crowns worth of new bonds are released, if necessary, in the counterbalancing open market sale by the central bank. Only $1/m$ times less worth of new bonds are released in such a counterbalancing process, as is described on pp. 49-52 of Sollenius (1996). Bond "transactions" between the central bank and the treasury have no relevance here at all, because, as mentioned in Step One, any interest income from the central bank is returned to the budget, hence those bonds given to the central bank can just as well be replaced, say, by a piece of paper telling about a 50-year noninterest loan.

To sum up our example: as a result of the counterbalancing open market sale the money supply is decreased by 100 million Crowns, back to the level before the whole story began. But in the meantime 100 million Crowns of face-value money created on paper "with a stroke of the pen" has been used to decrease the budget deficit, namely 100 million Crowns worth of interest burden on old bonds has been settled at the cost of selling only 10 million Crowns worth of new bonds.

However, there may be no need to counterbalance the released face-value money at all. Depending on the general economic situation in the country in question, in some cases the expansion of the money supply can be favourable or at least tolerable. For instance, the money supply increase may be in accord with the general goals of the government, since it may contribute to the monetary accomodation of an expansionist adjustment of the economy performed by fiscal measures (in a New Keynesian theoretical framework). In another case the money supply increase may be within the limits of the normal growth of the money supply for the economy in the given period (cf. pp. 57-60 in Sollenius 1996). In yet another case the possible raising of the interest rates on loans by the commercial banks to compensate themselves for believed losses of theoretical profits may also have advantageous consequences. Namely, such rises in market interest rates may automatically counterbalance the somewhat increased liquidity in the economy caused by the released amounts of face-value money due to monetization, hence no need arises for distinct counterbalancing measures.

In order to avoid overshooting in any direction, the release of the newly created money by means of TTs, and indeed the whole process of noninflationary monetization, should preferably be a gradual, step by step process. Even in cases when some measure of counterbalancing is unavoidable, the central bank should not force the commercial banks to perform a sudden process of deposit contraction by means of selling government bonds. This is unfavourable for two reasons. First, bond prices may then fall and this means that bond yields will rise, which after a while might raise the value of the average interest rate on the outstanding stock of public debt, denoted above as i; as a result monetization becomes more difficult and higher values of the proportion q will be necessary. Second, if the banks lose significant amounts of their valuable assets like government bonds, only to be replaced by weaker assets like the TTs, this influences their financial position unfavourably. Such side-effects may also result from counterbalancing by means of raised reserve requirements for the banks. For these reasons the monetizing actions under discussion should be performed with as little counterbalancing as possible, and if counterbalancing becomes inevitable, on further consideration the third method mentioned in Sollenius (1996:60-62): credit controls, may preferably be used.

For that matter, "credit rationing", according to Stiglitz and Weiss (1981), or "the allocation of credit", according to Mankiw (1986) seem to be favourite topics of authors within the New Keynesian trend of economics. Bernanke and Blinder (1988) even work out a model with "a distinct role for credit", that is, "bank loans", "a variant of the textbook IS-LM model", with the difference that their "model has three assets: money, bonds, and loans". Even today "government intervention into the allocation of credit is substantial", writes Mankiw (1986, reprinted in Mankiw and Romer 1991c:277). He concludes with the assertion that "(t)he federal government has played a central role in the allocation of credit among competing uses. ... At times, it is necessary for the government to remove some risk from the private sector by guaranteeing certain financial arrangements or, equivalently, by acting as a lender of last resort." (ibid., pp. 289-290).

Are credit controls not against the recent fashionable conservative trend of deregulation in the field of finance and banking? They certainly are. But today we are already living in a world ruled by banks, where welfare institutions are cut down and governments gasp for breath in the debt trap. A little more regulation and administrative control over the banking world given back to the democratically elected governments would enhance social justice and the general welfare of people.

EXTERNAL PUBLIC DEBT

If the government - and the central bank co-operating with it - give priority to fighting unemployment, they can well include the foreign-owed part of the public debt in the circle of monetization; in this way they will meet no obstacle to increasing the proportion of the monetized part of the yearly interest burden on the stock of public debt, to a higher level, somewhat closer to 1, if necessary. For paying interest on the debt to foreign creditors, not the TTs but simply the traditional way of monetization can, of course, be used; the above formula for q is then slightly different.

For example, the central bank simply creates money, sends it to the treasury, which buys the necessary foreign exchange abroad (possibly through intermediaries) and pays the interest to the foreign creditors. This process may cause a measure of depreciation of the domestic currency against the foreign currency in question, but this only benefits the goals of increasing exports, stimulating domestic growth and fighting domestic unemployment. The rate of domestic inflation may increase somewhat due to the small de facto devaluation, but, as has been said, the goal of fighting inflation in this situation can be considered secondary. Anyway, in some cases a rise in domestic interest rates might accompany the processes of monetization under discussion, and this might lead to some capital inflow from abroad which can at least partially compensate for the initial depreciation of the domestic currency resulting from the purchase of foreign exchange.

The act of money creation and the purchase of foreign exchange might lead to some economic consequences abroad, but if the acts described are performed in a small country, the effects are usually negligible. If they are performed in a large country, then the possible economic consequences abroad need a careful, case-by-case analysis. The necessary foreign exchange could also be purchased within the home country, but in this case a manoeuvre of "sterilization", that is, the sale of a package of bonds with an equivalent value performed by the central bank would be needed in order to counteract the ensuing change in the domestic money supply, and the sale of new bonds does not serve our purpose in this case.

The suggested method of monetizing the external part of the public debt means that this part of the annual interest burden practically represents zero expense when we set out to construct a theoretical "monetized" interest rate. But even some other parts of the ostensible annual interest burden of the outstanding public debt can be taken into consideration with zero value, and this way of viewing the debt problem is also significant.

DEBT WITHIN THE PUBLIC SECTOR

The Maastricht Treaty can be criticized with justification on many accounts, but it certainly succeeded at least in defining the notion of the consolidated public sector as regards the calculation of debt. As the "Protocol on the excessive deficit procedure" states: "government means general government, that is central government, regional or local government and social security funds, to the exclusion of commercial operations". Furthermore, "debt means total gross debt at nominal value outstanding at the end of the year and consolidated between and within the sectors of general government as defined in the first indent", that is, in our previous sentence here (see, for instance, Venables 1992:cxlv-cxlvi). The significance of this principle should not be underestimated.

We are now using this logical and apt definition to illustrate the idea according to which there need be no concern about interest payments on the debt between and within parts of the consolidated public sector, that is, government in the wider sense. Countries with large public sectors and large social insurance funds, for instance, the West European welfare states in general, and Sweden in particular, obviously have some advantage here. Indeed, interest on the debt owed to various parts of the public sector never has to be actually "paid out"; it can always remain a matter of figures on a piece of paper. The direction and influence of central government in economic decisions can ensure that these amounts always remain on paper. Maturing debt and any interest on it can be replaced endlessly by new bonds without any expense, except the printing costs, of course, but those are accounted for under other headings. And what is burden on one side of the public sector is revenue on the other side. In a way the whole public sector can be viewed as a system which enhances its own wealth by the interest revenue on the bonds owed by one part of it to another. The central bank should obviously be included in the public sector, and as an internal engine, it can always be ready to monetize in one way or another if necessary. When calculating a theoretical "monetized" interest rate on the outstanding debt in order to determine the paths of growth of the self-multiplicating burden of the debt, those parts of the annual interest burden owed between and within parts of the consolidated public sector can in fact be taken into consideration even at the very worst as having zero value, let alone viewing them as revenue.

As we will explain in more detail later, the whole "interest" game is basically a "market" phenomenon, and the public sector, so to say, upsets the whole game. There is no need whatsoever to place any part of these processes within the public sector as a burden on the taxpayer.

We remain with the zero value mentioned above and denote as q_z the proportion of all such parts of the annual interest burden that for one reason or another can be taken into consideration with zero value. It is more or less the same if q_z is calculated as the summarized amount of the debt with zero interest burden divided by the whole debt, and naturally the result is a figure between 0 and 1. Modifying our previous formulas accordingly, we can now write that:

$$i_m = c \cdot i(1-q_z-q) + 0 \cdot q_z + j \cdot q \ .$$

The medium term with zero value is the most important factor here, of course. From this we get the following for the critical, stabilizing value of the proportion of the yearly interest burden monetized with TTs, that is, q in the new situation:

$$q = (c.i/1-q_z/ - i_o) / (c.i - j) \text{ or}$$

$$q = (i_r/1-q_z/ - i_o) / (i_r - j) .$$

Every symbol is the same here as earlier, the only difference being that a factor of $/1-q_z/$ is introduced. As a consequence, however, we can now easily get a negative value for q, which means that there is no need for any interference with releasing TTs, because q_z, the zero-value part of the interest burden, can manage to stabilize the debt alone. Indeed, if a welfare state has a large public sector, and if in addition the interest burden on its foreign debt can be monetized bravely in the way described above, then q_z can easily be as high as, for instance, 0.6 to 0.65 . In such a country only those parts of the annual interest burden on the public debt which are owed to private banks and other private financial institutions, e.g. private insurance companies, as well as to the nonbank public, including households and private enterprises, should be considered a hard nut to crack. Sometimes the aggregate proportion of all these lenders of the state debt may be only up to about 35 to 40 percent of the whole debt (cf., for instance, the case of the Swedish national debt in Tab. 276 of Statistics Sweden 1995:248).

But there may remain the problem of accurately calculating the further nominal growth of the outstanding public debt. We recall that within the public sector we tacitly accepted ongoing bond financing of the debt without any real costs for the annual budget balance. But the results of the bond-financing process still nominally increase the outstanding stock of the debt if this is accounted for in the conventional way (cf. ibid., for example). The solution could be another way of accounting for the debt, even when the same methods described above are applied. Instead of introducing q_z we can use the earlier formulas, but we define ways of taking into consideration only certain parts of the outstanding stock of debt. For instance, if foreign debt is monetized in the way described above and the public sector debt is bond-financed free of expense, then one can define a lower level of "effective" debt, hence a lower kind of b, only taking into consideration the private sector internal debt and its ratio to the GDP. In this case a higher i_o will result and the stabilization of the lower effective debt stock will be considerably easier even at higher rates of interest.

MONETIZATION IN GENERAL

The question can be raised whether it is sound and fair to use any 'financial tricks' at all, as we have described, to create money out of nothing. Can they not be abused? Indeed, some forms of monetization with the outlay of high-powered money and increasing the domestic money supply could lead to inflation if they were abused, that is, applied without limits. The first mentioned noninflationary method is more difficult to abuse because on the domestic scene it only releases face-value money in the form of TTs and has its counterbalancing processes if needed. But, of course, this does not mean that it can be applied without restrictions; naturally it has its limitations. Mere money creation cannot generally replace productive economic activities in society, and on a much more modest and prosaic scale: unrestricted application of the method may place too heavy a burden on the banking system. But the new method can be recommended at least as a means of breaking the vicious circle of contemporary debt-accumulation, which is a sort of 'debt trap' or 'debt sclerosis'. It can be used to alleviate the currently growing interest burden of the accumulated stocks of public debt, to stabilize and later perhaps gradually erode these debt stocks themselves.

When considering the justification of using such 'tricks', it must be realized that the accumulation of compound interest on past public debt is an unfortunate trick itself; it is unsound in the first place. Compound interest on past public debt no longer has any direct connection with the real economy, with present production; it is alien to the real economic process of the present. It is the automatic creation of money, of liabilities in money, out of nothing, by the mere passing of time.

A very fashionable basic element of the prevalent economic philosophy nowadays is the following idea: make the state just another participant in the economic game, an actor in the market like anyone else. Subordinate the budgetary activities of the state "to the control of the market". All that is "public" is wrong or at best doubtful, all that is "market" is good. The state has to pay the interest on its past borrowings rigorously, under every circumstance, whatever happens. According to such a mentality, the bond-holders would have to receive their due interest even if the normal life of society broke down and masses of people suffered, even if society came to a standstill.

Such fashionable ideas are the ultimate cause of the contemporary debt sclerosis. When considering interest on capital, a distinction must be made between the case of individual participants in the economic game and the case of society as a whole. (Here I regard even one country as 'society', as a self-sufficient entity, because I do not favour foreign indebtedness. But the same reasoning is also valid for the world economy as a whole.) Individual participants in the economic game charge interest on loans to each other; one pays it, the other receives it, at the end it is a zero-sum game. If one enterprise cannot pay, it goes bankrupt and others take its place. But the case of a whole society is different. Society as a whole must not go bankrupt.

Interest on the part of society as a whole can only be paid normally from an increase in society's production, if it can be paid at all. The notion of interest in this case has to be considered in relation to production. In reality "interest" only makes sense if there is a real increase in goods and services, in other words, if there is a surplus as a result of production. The notion of interest paid by society as a whole only makes sense if there is growth, high enough to cover the new liabilities created out of nothing, by the mere passing of time.

But what about a 'pedagogical' type of reasoning that might read like this: governments' burdens of public debts and budget deficits should never be alleviated. Governments should always be kept under pressure in order to find better management methods that generate economic growth. Such rigorous conservative reasoning, which treats governments like lazy school-children, misses the point that lower growth rates in most advanced industrial countries today may well be caused not merely by lack of diligence or talent of governments, but probably by historical, structural factors. In addition, low contemporary growth rates are certainly perpetuated by the debt sclerosis, the debt trap itself.

As Andersson et al. (1996:20-21) reveal, in recent decades, "during the process of deflation within the EU the real interest rate has not fallen, but risen. ... Since Germany's monetary policy started to dominate the rest of Europe's the real interest rate has settled permanently on average at about 5 per cent for Europe." As a consequence, the (r-y) difference, mentioned by Sollenius (1996:18 ff.) following the analysis by Dornbusch and Fischer (1990:614, 628), has often become higher today in several European countries compared to previous decades. (For Sweden in 2000 it may be about 2 to 3 percent.) But for society as a whole, considered as a self-sufficient entity of production and consumption, the abstract notion of "interest" is only reasonable as long as its rate does not exceed the rate of increase, during the same time, of society's aggregate output of production.

For less critical connections between interest and the sphere of production see, for instance, Wicksell (1936:102-156) and Wicksell (1898, reprinted in 1958:78-89) about the "natural rate of interest", and also Hicks (1977:65) about the "real return on investment, the productivity, in terms of real goods, of the inputs on which the borrowed money is to be spent", when he analyses Wicksell's ideas (ibid., pp. 61-72).

At the very moment when r becomes greater than y, that is to say, when the real interest rate exceeds the real growth rate, the growing interest burden on society as a whole becomes, so to say, fictive, unreal; it becomes a vicious trick, the revenge of one of our invented notions inflicted on ourselves. Then the interest burden created from nothing grows faster than our ability to bear it. At that very moment the application of some reasonable 'counter-tricks' becomes entirely justified.

Domestic private bond-holders should get their money, but not at the cost of people's suffering. For instance, in the first mentioned method of noninflationary monetization new face-value money is created on paper and distributed to the bond-holders by sending out TTs to the banking system. If necessary, such a manoeuvre can be counterbalanced by an open market sale or by some credit controls in order to prevent extra inflation. Liabilities automatically created from nothing by the passing of time could be settled with money deliberately created from nothing, if no significant increase in inflation is caused. In times of recession, when it becomes politically untenable to squeeze out ever greater primary surpluses from the people by austerity measures, some methods of noninflationary monetization might prove to be a way out of the debt trap for some countries.

Noninflationary monetization can be useful during periods of governmental efforts to decrease unemployment. In contrast with fashionable contemporary beliefs about the absolute superiority of the "market" and the private sector - a conservative Utopia - the truth is that owing to technological development, rises in productivity and rationalization, the private sector in advanced, industrialized societies may only be able to create a limited number of lasting new jobs even in the best economic boom. At the same time our modern, industrialized societies require a growing amount of welfare services, jobs in education and health care, in care of the young, the old and the sick. These services cannot be extensively privatized, first because most recipients are usually not capable of exerting effective control over the quality, price and conditions of private services, and second because the privatization of such services greatly increases social inequality. Hence the problem of unemployment in our advanced Western societies can only be solved definitively with powerful public sector support (cf. also Berglund 1996:83-85 and 110-112, in particular).

However, "direct monetization", the first-mentioned method of noninflationary monetization is too vulnerable to be used to finance a combined Keynesian expansion, due to the possible accumulation of too many TTs in the banking system. For a combined Keynesian expansion the notion of "noninflationary monetization" should be interpreted in the widest sense, simply as "monetization without inflation". This question is examined further in the next chapter.

PRUDENT MONETARY EXPANSION

SMALL-STEP MONETIZATION

Governments and public authorities are expected to be very cautious when trying out some new, unusual or supposedly risky ideas; we therefore now attempt to suggest a cautious version of monetization for the purpose of financing a combined Keynesian expansion to create new jobs within the public sector. To determine a reasonably cautious size of a needed monetary expansion we propose the following: monetize in small steps, each time within the yearly target ranges of the money supply growth recommended by contemporary experts.

Now let us look at a simple example, for which the rough numbers are taken from contemporary Swedish economic conditions. Suppose that the government intends to decrease a six and a half percent open unemployment level (with about 260,000 openly unemployed) by two and a half percent, that is, by about 100,000 persons, to the four percent level (about 160,000 remaining openly unemployed) during a period of one year. To do so it intends to create 100,000 new jobs within the welfare services provided by the public sector, with on average about the equivalent salary of a hospital orderly ("sjukvardsbiträde") or an assistant nurse ("undersköterska"), that is, health service workers without higher qualifications. For that matter, according to Statistics Sweden (1998:105), in the early 2000s just about 100,000 new workers with these low qualifications will be badly needed in the Swedish public health service system. By public sector we mean here what the definition in the Maastricht Treaty refers to by the expression "consolidated public sector" (see Venables 1992).

The government will only have to pay the after-tax difference between the average yearly salary of an assistant nurse (or a health service worker without higher qualification) and the average yearly unemployment benefit of 80 percent of the same size of salary. This fact, in a reversed form, namely in connection with firing municipal workers, and further reducing the difference with the amount of housing benefit ("bostadsbidrag"), is also pointed out by Sten Johansson, with his words registered by Ekdahl (1999). Also Modigliani et al. (1998:18) admit that "a government stimulus to aggregate demand (and thereby vacancies) could ... be financed, partially or wholly, through the associated drop in unemployment benefit payments". According to Esping-Andersen (1995:26; 1996b:70), unemployment benefit in several European countries is roughly within the same range as in Sweden.

Taxation is approximately the same for both a low earned salary and an unemployment benefit, say, about 30 percent in tax (mainly municipal), so both should be reduced by this. Payroll tax and other kinds of employer's contributions all go back to the big purse of the public sector, so we do not have to bother about them. Suppose the yearly salary of an assistant nurse is on average about 180,000 Swedish Crowns before tax. Then the government needs 0.2 times 0.7 times 180,000 times 100,000 Crowns, which makes 2.52 billion Crowns of additional money to be monetized in order to create the 100,000 new jobs.

As has been said, this additional money should be created for the government by the central bank, after the rules forbidding such a measure are eliminated in Sweden, as well as hopefully in the whole European Union, for instance, by changing the Maastricht Treaty. Would such a comparatively small amount of monetized additional budgetary outlay do any harm? Would it be inflationary? Suppose for a moment that we are the followers of Friedman's (1968:16) monetarist rule of "something like a 3 to 5 per cent per year rate of growth in currency plus all commercial bank deposits" to be kept "steady". According to Sveriges Riksbank (1999:74), the M3 monetary aggregate in Sweden at the end of November 1999 was approximately 916 billion Crowns. Bank reserve requirements ("kassakraven") in Sweden were reduced to zero back in the spring of 1994 (Sveriges Riksbank 1995:45), and in consequence the 2.52 billion Crowns created newly by the central bank will not be high-powered money, merely face-value money. This means that, viewing the M3 money aggregate, the 2.52 billion additional supply of face-value money represents only about 0.3 percent additional growth of the money supply. Even by monetarist standards this can be regarded as negligible.

But in order to see the 0.3 percent change of the money supply in proportion to the contemporary practice of monetary regulation, let us look at what size of money growth is proposed, for instance, by the Federal Open Market Committee in the United States as a target range for growth of the M3 money aggregate. According to Daane (1994:142-143), "the ranges for monetary policy" as regards the growth of the M3 monetary aggregate in both 1991 and 1992 were 1 to 5 percent growth and in 1993 it was 0.5 to 4.5 percent growth. We have no reason to suppose that such ranges are narrower in the late 1990s or early 2000s. One can realize that an additional 0.3 percent upward change in the growth of the M3 money aggregate may comfortably fall within the fairly wide recommendable ranges of money supply growth, and this can be true in a European country just as well. Even ten times more money could be monetized comfortably, which in our Swedish example would mean up to one million more jobs created in a year within the public sector. Thus a governmental action accomplishing a combined Keynesian expansion of a similar size cannot be regarded as leading to inflationary consequences in Sweden.

As regards the United States, the above assessment using the difference between the full salary and the 80 percent unemployment benefit is not valid. According to the U. S. Bureau of the Census (1997:370), "(s)tate laws vary concerning the length of time benefits are paid and their amount". According to statistical figures (ibid.,

p. 382, table No. 595), in 1995 only 34.8 percent of the civilian unemployed had insured unemployment, and the size of the average unemployment benefit was only 35.5 percent of the average weekly wage. If one reckons with paying the whole 100 percent salary of those entering the new low-qualification health service jobs mentioned, instead of merely the 20 percent difference between the full salary and the unemployment benefit, then this means a five times greater amount of money required and to be created by the central bank. If we suppose all other conditions and figures to be similar between the two countries, just for the sake of a rough assessment, then this would mean 5 times about 0.3 percent, that is, about 1.5 percent increment of the M3 monetary aggregate. This figure can still fall comfortably within the fairly wide recommendable ranges of money supply growth, which, as emphasized, can be supposed to be similar even in the late 1990s and early 2000s to those described for the early 1990s by Daane (1994:142-143). Provided there is a similarity between the two countries in conditions and circumstances, a similar but in absolute job numbers proportionally larger, governmentally induced combined Keynesian expansion to decrease unemployment by two and a half percent could also be performed in the United States, without the risk of the accompanying act of monetization leading to inflationary consequences.

ENDOGENOUS MONEY SUPPLY

Besides comparing the percentage size of money growth with the broad target ranges for the growth of money aggregates determined by the Federal Open Market Committee in the United States, it is also possible to make other calculations to assess the consequences of "arbitrary" money creation. In theory one can broadly assess that the results of monetizing a combined Keynesian expansion (CKE) may become inflationary or not, by comparing the amount or the relative proportion of newly created money with the amount or the relative proportion of brand new money needed to serve the greater transactions demand for money due to the higher level of output, that is, income.

In order to assess the percentage increment in output we turn to Keynes's (1936:113-131) well-known concept of the multiplier, about which he himself reveals (ibid., p. 113) that "(t)he conception of the multiplier was first introduced into economic theory by Mr. R. F. Kahn in his article on 'The Relation of Home Investment to Unemployment' (Economic Journal, June 1931)". Keynes first distinguished between what he called the "investment multiplier", which he defined as the ratio of the amount of increase in income to the "increment of aggregate investment" that caused it, and the "employment multiplier", of which he said that "it measures the ratio of the increment of total employment which is associated with a given increment of primary employment in the investment industries" (ibid., p. 115). He said (ibid.) that originally "Mr. Kahn's multiplier" was "what we may call the employment multiplier" and it is "a little different from" the investment multiplier. But Keynes (ibid., pp. 115-116) added that although "there is no reason in general to suppose" that the two are equal, "(i)f ... there is no reason to expect any material relevant difference in the shapes of the aggregate supply functions for industry as a whole and for the investment industries respecively," then the two can be considered equal.

For our rough assessment we also suppose the latter case, that is, one common multiplier value. But first we should turn to Dornbusch and Fischer (1990:98-99 and 103-105) to make sure that what we are dealing with is not a "balanced budget multiplier", the value of which is said to be always only 1. Since the increase in demand by the government in our above example is not financed by tax increases but by monetization, we should not bother with what is generally called "balanced budget multiplier", even though the CKE we suggest will not actually burden the government's budget, so that it can remain unchanged, that is, balanced, in the first instance. We can simply make our assessment with what is today generally called the Keynesian multiplier, the value of which is taken as $1 / (1-c)$, where c is the slope of the consumption function. In theoretical examples c is usually between 0.6 and 0.8 today, and this gives multipliers between 2.5 and 5 (cf. Dornbusch and Fischer 1990:78-98). Berglund (1996:83) calculates a multiplier value of 6.72 on increasing internal public sector demand in Sweden in the 1990s, which is very close to our case. But let us be modest and suppose a multiplier value of only 2.5 for our above Swedish example.

Returning to the figures of the example of creating 100,000 new jobs in the Swedish public health service, let us consider the 2.52 billion Crowns to be monetized to cover the difference between salaries and unemployment benefits as "investment". Then with a multiplier value of 2.5 we get 6.3 billion as increment in output. Since the extrapolated, assessed value of the Swedish BNP by about the year 2000 will be around 1800 billion Crowns (cf., for instance, Statistics Sweden 1999:235, Tab. 264), the 6.3 billion increment in output would mean about 0.35 percent growth. Then we use the "square root law of the demand for money", described by Dornbusch and Fischer (1990:354-360), referring to the results of Baumol (1952) and Tobin (1956) about the calculation of the transactions demand for money. The "income elasticity of the demand for money" is about 1/2, say Dornbusch and Fischer (1990:360), which in fact approximately corresponds to the square root with small increments. This gives 0.35/2, that is, 0.175 percent as growth in the transactions demand for money.

Comparing the approximately 0.3 percent increase in the money supply required for the monetization of the CKE performed by the government, it is possible to say that it is somewhat higher than the growth in the transactions demand for money, o.175. However, in addition to those motives for holding money which today are summed up under the heading of the transactions demand for money, Keynes (1936:194-209) also distinguished "the Precautionary motive" and "the Speculative motive" as further reasons for money demand. We have no exact calculus to determine the sizes of these components of the money demand, but they may be supposed to cover the tiny difference between the approximately 0.3 percent money supply growth accompanying the CKE at issue and the 0.175 percent increase in the transactions demand for money, calculated on the basis of the idea of considering the 2.52 billion Crowns newly created money as new "investment". But even apart from the other two motives of money demand, the whole size of the difference here, the 0.125 percent in money growth, is so small that it could not be regarded as leading to inflationary consequences of any significance.

In addition, one could take into consideration the fact that a rather modest multiplier value of 2.5 was chosen, and, on the other hand, we took the theoretical income elasticity of 1/2 concerning the transactions demand for money. Dornbusch and Fischer (1990:370-371) cite the empirical results of Small and Porter (1989) based on data between 1961 and 1988, according to which the long-run income elasticity of M2 money demand was 1.03. Calculating with such an elasticity for our M3 too, we would get about a 0.35 percent increase in the money demand, which is just slightly higher than the 0.3

percent growth in the money supply, and then inflationary consequences are obviously out of the question.

As regards the similar imaginary example in the case of the United States, also mentioned earlier, there the differences between full salaries and unemployment benefits are considerably greater, and fewer people have benefits. Therefore, even if a fivefold upward reassessment, corresponding to the difference between 20 percent and 100 percent, disregarding unemployment benefits completely, is not needed, about three or four times more money could still be required for the CKE mentioned. On the other hand, a more realistic, higher multiplier could also be chosen, and then the money demand is also twice or three times higher. On balance such kinds of assessments would probably result in a somewhat higher money supply growth than money demand growth in the case of a similar example referring to the United States, but the difference would still be only once or twice the size of the 0.3 percent originally mentioned money supply growth, that is, still a rather small increment, with no significant inflationary effects.

Perhaps the time spent on bothering about the possibility or not of inflationary consequences of a CKE financed entirely by monetization, was wasted time. According to serious views in Post Keynesian Macroeconomics it is not necessary to make a problem of this question, because the money supply in modern economies has thoroughly endogenous characteristics, accomodating money demand and ultimately output.

It is worth quoting a brief opinion of Galbraith and Darity (1994:440) on this idea, which we consider the most important contribution of PKM to the general debate in economics: "Some post-Keynesians believe that the money supply is endogenous and that monetary authorities are obliged to supply whatever quantity of money is demanded. ... loans are made automatically as borrowers increase their demand for money. In general, the monetary authorities accomodate the swings in money demand. A more or less effective policy consistent with this viewpoint is to control interest rates ...."

According to Sherman and Evans (1984:318), "(t)o say that the money stock is endogenous means that the magnitude of whatever serves as money in some sense depends upon other activities in the economy over which the monetary authorities have little direct control. Money is a dependent variable." Such an argument, they say, "shatters the monetarist paradigm, which "depends entirely upon the notion that the Fed controls money". There, "(i)n monetarism, money demand adjusts to the controlled money supply through price changes" (ibid., p.319).

But the "endogenous" argument, which is "antithetical to the monetarist perspective", Sherman and Evans (ibid.) say, "insists on the opposite: in the long run, the supply of money adjusts to the demand for money. Money responds to the ... needs of trade." If the central bank "refuses to accomodate this impulse, then innovative entrepreneurs will eventually modify the institutional structure" and produce new instruments which begin "to serve as money".

Sherman and Evans (1984:319-320) point out that the "notion of the endogenous money stock goes back at least as far as Adam Smith", who "provided the image of entrepreneurs devising their own medium of circulation when conventional sources refused to accomodate their needs". In contrast, Ricardo rather accepted the quantity theory of money, the archetype of monetarism, and throughout the 19th century, apart from a debate about the Bank of England in the 1840s, the endogenous idea was rarely raised. But in the 20th century "many of those who have followed (the Keynesian) tradition ... have brought back the notion of the endogenous money supply" (ibid., p. 320). After referring to the views in the Report of the Radcliffe Committee that "(a)ll financial assets have the monetary quality in varying degrees", Sherman and Evans (ibid.) quote Nicholas Kaldor's (1970) claim that "any shortage of money is bound to lead to the emergence of new types". They also mention Minsky's views and enlist "(s)ome examples of ... 'financial innovation'", such as "money market mutual funds, the commercial paper market, federal funds market, the repurchase agreement markets". Referring to Tobin's and Laidler's views, they conclude that "(e)ntrepreneurs innovate in the financial sector as well" as in any other areas, and thus the "money supply cannot be controlled in the long run", according to these views (ibid., p. 321).

Sherman and Evans (1984:322, 323 and 324) point at some well-known examples of how the money supply takes on endogenous characteristics: how banks "aggressively use the discount window" at the Fed to borrow reserves and how they frequently use the federal funds market to get reserves by overnight repurchase agreements, as well as how banks shift the composition of their deposit liabilities in favour of more "nonmonetary" assets, for instance, certificates of deposit, in order to lower reserve requirements and free reserves. The reason for all these phenomena is the changed behaviour of banks from "the image of the 'passive' banker", who "would accept loan business only if reserves are available" to "modern banking", to "(l)arge banks" which "today aggressively solicit loan business", and do not "turn away ... valued customers when loans are requested merely because their reserve position is tight". Therefore the "loans are often made and the reserves are worried about later", Sherman and Evans (ibid., p. 323) explain.

It is true that the "ability of banks to circumvent the Fed's goals is still restrained ...There is a limit to how far banks can go. But the banks do have a great deal of latitude, and if loan demand is volatile, then bank lending and the money supply will also be volatile even if ultimately constrained by limits. At least in this sense ... the money supply is endogenous, that is, determined by economic activity and the demand ... rather than by the Federal Reserve System", Sherman and Evans conclude (ibid., pp. 324-325).

Perhaps this is the right place to recall that in Sweden the reserve requirements for banks, called "kassakraven", were reduced to zero in the spring of 1994 (see Sveriges Riksbank 1995:45). For this reason it is much more difficult in Sweden for the central bank to influence the money supply, and in consequence the money supply can take on endogenous characteristics much more easily than in many other countries.

Ingham (1998:7) says that while "post-Keynesian monetary analysis focuses on the autonomous role of banks in the creation of 'endogenous' credit-money in capitalism", he goes "a little further by suggesting that this production of bank-credit (and state-credit) money is a constitutive feature of capitalism". He asserts that "the distinctive character of capitalist banking lies in the creation of credit-money", that is, "in the capacity to 'manufacture' money through the act of lending and the creation of new deposits". Later he again points out the significance of the "'credit' theory (of banking practice) that 'loans make deposits'" instead of vice versa, and hence "this relatively autonomous production of credit-money makes possible ever more complex sytems of production and exchange" (ibid., p. 11).

According to Galbraith and Darity's (1994:394) summary of the "post-Keynesian" view, in order to get reserves for giving loans, "banks borrow reserves from other banks. If the banking system as a whole is short of reserves, the federal funds rate (the rate on interbank lending of reserves) will rise. The central bank, seeing this, will react by adding reserves to the system. The money supply therefore rises and falls as much as borrowers, as a group, choose that it should.". Indeed, this is a very clear summary of how those central banks watching primarily the interest rate behave today, we can add.

Hillier (1991:72n-73n) says about the criticism of monetarism that it "often goes along the lines that the money supply actually is, and has been, endogenous". Also when speaking about "interest rate targeting", Hillier (1991:97n) says that "the government allows the money supply to adjust to maintain a fixed interest rate" and he refers to Kaldor and Trevithick (1981) for a discussion of the endogeneity of the money supply.

Rousseas (1986:ix) sums up his view as follows: "... the two major schools of monetary policy were the neoclassical Keynesians with their IS-LM models of fine-tuning, and the monetarists who started their rapid climb to dominance in the 1960s. Post Keynesian monetary economics rejects both of these both of these approaches and it does so largely by reversing the causal arrow of the quantity theory of money. The money supply is seen as a function of nominal income rather than the other way around. What this amounts to is an endogenous theory of the money supply."

Later Rousseas (ibid., pp. 79-80) quotes Kaldor's (1980) work and in particular Kaldor's (1982) view that "'... at all times, the money stock will be determined by demand, and the rate of interest determined by the Central Bank'". As he elaborates: "the money supply is endogenous and demand-driven while the rate of interest (the bank rate) is the exogenously determined basic price of money set and administered by the central bank. This constitutes a complete reversal of traditional monetary theory." Returning to Kaldor he repeats that "the money supply ... is 'dependent on demand, governed by the level of income' and which the central bank must accomodate as lender of last resort if the collapse of the financial system is to be avoided".

According to Rousseas's (ibid., p. 80) explanation of Kaldor's theory, "(t)he demand for money ... is a function of nominal income and changes in the demand for money are the result of 'changes in the level of production and income' brought about by changes in the rate of interest. ... The causal scenarion runs as follows: a fall in the rate of interest causes an increase in investment which, in turn, causes income to rise by some multiple of the increase in investment. This increase in income results in an increased demand for transactions balances which, at a given bank rate, is met by the central bank acting as a lender of last resort to the banks."

Galbraith and Darity (1994:395) say, in accordance with the above, that "Post-Keynesians believe ... that it is not appropriate to represent the money supply curve as an exogenous policy instrument or as the vertical line characteristic of the monetarist model. The post-Keynesian money supply schedule is horizontal, as shown in Figure 12.2.". This figure shows the "Interest Rate" on the vertical axis and the "Money Stock" on the horizontal axis (ibid., p. 395). In the Post Keynesian view the interest rate is fixed, shown with a horizontal line, and the money supply is not fixed, but determined by the crossing point of the fixed horizontal interest rate line and the negatively sloped money demand curve. As the explanation to the figure says: "...the central bank sets the interest rate and lets money demand determine money supply", according to the Post Keynesian view.

Sherman and Evans (1984:322) discuss the theory of B. Moore (1979 and 1981), which says that in case of demands for bank loans, "(i)f no reserves are available, pressure is applied to the Federal Reserve System to provide more reserves. The Fed understands that their failure to act might produce unemployment ... which the Fed regards as intolerable. Consequently, they relent, allowing the loans to be made." In other words, "the money supply is essentially 'politically endogenous', the Fed relents because of the political pressures imposed by unemployment". Sherman and Evans add that the "(m)onetarists, in fact, might agree with Moore's theory. They would simply insist ... that the Fed should not relent ..." (ibid.).

According to Sherman and Evans (1984:322), "credit market stabilization policy" is the "primary mandate" of the Fed, and not, as "(i)t may seem", the "singular function" "to control inflation". "A credit market stabilization policy ... has two objectives: keep interest rate volatility to a minimum, and keep interest rates low." - Sherman and Evans (ibid., pp. 322-323) say. In consequence, "when growing credit demand causes interest rates to rise, the Fed, in the effort to stabilize the rates, will conduct an expansionary open market operation. ... This act provides the banks with more reserves, which allows an expansion of bank loans (and money)." Sherman and Evans (ibid., p. 323) conclude that "the very policy mechanism itself will ensure that money will be forthcoming to meet the short-run demand of bank-credit money".

Indeed, this is how the Fed works today. The endogeneity of the money supply obviously depends decisively on the behaviour of the central bank. When we earlier referred to Sternlight's (1994:116-117) illustration, even in figures, of "Levels and Targets (Cones and Tunnels)" of various monetary aggregates, as well as Daane's (1994:143) description in a table of "Ranges of Growth of Monetary and Credit Aggregates", it might have been supposed that these - fairly wide - ranges, levels and targets were some kind of monetarist, rulist prescriptions. But this is not the case. These ranges belong only to one of the sixteen types of "Intermediate Policy Indicators (Targets)" which are enlisted by Jones (1994:87, Figure 7.1) as factors referred to in the text (ibid., p. 86) as "a myriad of intermediate indicators to be used in determining when Fed policy shifts are appropriate". About these the Fed gathers all available information in order to get a picture of the current economic situation in the country, before making any decision.

The really important factors for the Fed lie hidden among the "Alternative Operating Procedures (Guidelines)", which are only three: the "Federal Funds Rate", the "Borrowed Reserves" and the "Nonborrowed Reserves" (ibid., p.87). According to Jones (ibid., p. 95), "(u)ntil

1979 the Fed ... focused exclusively on the Fed funds rate as its operating guideline. ... From 1979 to 1982 the Fed targeted the supply of nonborrowed reserves. From 1982 to 1987, the Fed focused primarily on a borrowings guideline. Since 1987, the Greenspan Fed has focused on twin operating guidelines: borrowings and the Fed funds rate." Jones (ibid., p. 96) emphasizes again that today the "Fed has joint operating guidelines of the Fed funds rate and borrowed reserves". This is very important to stress, indeed, because from these facts it is evident that nonborrowed reserves, that is, the great bulk of the total reserves in the banking system, were among the operating guidelines only between 1979 and 1982. This was the brief period when the Fed was under the influence of the then victorious monetarist theory.

Today the Fed obviously does not care any longer about the monetarist favourites: the monetary base and the money supply growth. But what does the Fed really care about? It turns out from the words of Jones (ibid., pp. 95-100) that among the remaining two guidelines the borrowed reserves are today merely indicators, even if "the most sensitive indicators of changes in Fed policy" (ibid., p. 98). The real aim of the Fed is to regulate the Fed funds rate, which "is the key short-term interest rate for all the financial markets" (ibid., p. 95). Jones (ibid., p. 99) explains it again: "In essence, the Fed funds rate represents the primary cost of short-term loanable funds and will influence the prime bank lending rate. The Fed's primary impact is usually on short-term rates, but at times longer-term rates will follow suit. These are costs to borrowers. Changing these interest rates will then affect aggregate demand ...".

Sternlight (1994:111) reveals the same process by saying that through open market operations the Fed seeks to affect "the degree of pressure or tension in the market for reserves. That degree of pressure exerts a major impact on the Fed funds rate, which is the overnight rate on bank reserves, and through that rate has an influence throughout the short-term money market and eventually the entire spectrum of interest rates." By open market operations the Fed wants "to determine the degree of pressure, and hence the rate level, in the federal funds market" (ibid., p. 112).

Thus the Fed's main goal is to regulate and keep at the regulated level the interest rates in the country. As a means to this aim, it conducts as many open market sales or purchases of bonds as necessary, which, by the way, also influences the total amount of reserves in the banking system and hence the money supply. Through its open market operations the Fed in fact flexibly accomodates the money supply as a means of regulating and keeping the interest rate at the regulated level. The Fed works today precisely by making the money supply endogenous, that is, freely accomodating to economic demand for money, in order to ensure that the interest rate, primarily the Fed funds rate, is kept fixed at a carefully considered, from time to time slightly regulated level. This means that before 1979 and since 1987 again the money supply in the United States was and is essentially endogenous. And so is it in some other countries in the industrialized world, wherever the central banks have as their main task to focus on keeping the interest rates at required fixed levels.

The fact that such an economic policy can be very successful is well illustrated by the case of the United States in the 1990s. In addition to the two main, general causal factors originating in world politics and technological development, mentioned earlier, a third, specific factor contributing to the long-lasting boom in the economy of the U. S. during most of the 1990s was the clever policies of the Fed under the chairmanship of Alan Greenspan since 1987. Right at the outset, at the time of the October 1987 stock market crash, the Greenspan Fed averted a major financial crisis by quickly assuring the public that it firmly stood by its role as the lender of last resort, and provided enough money to forestall a panic. Ever since it has mostly pursued policies on balance leaning in a more or less Keynesian direction. The result is that, as Dornbusch, Fischer and Startz (1998:428-429) explicitly put it, "(t)here can be no doubt that in the 1990s active and discretionary Fed policy, a fine-tuning policy, has helped keep the economy operating better than at any time in the last 30 years. ... on balance, the Fed has done an excellent job."

Some critics might raise the objection that such a way of allowing the endogenous accomodation of the money supply to regulate and maintain the level of the interest rate only functions well as long as the purpose is to lower or to keep the rate low. But what will happen if, in order to restrain inflationary pressures in the short run, it becomes necessary to raise the interest rate level by decreasing the money supply via open market operations? Will then the ensuing relative money shortage and the rise of the interest rates not mean a kind of "crowding out" for the private sector? Incidentally, since such a decrease of the money supply is initiated by the Fed, one might question whether, in this case, the restrictive change in the money supply is "exogenous" or, since in the process of regulating the interest rate the changing of bank reserves is only instrumental, the downward accomodating money supply - as a by-product - can rightly be called endogenous.

The answer to the "crowding out" question in this case may in part be the argument that, as the example of the Fed in the 1990s showed, the contractional, deflationary phases in the process of interest rate regulation can be subtle enough not to cause significant crowding out. The other part of the answer may be the reference to some other possible ways of restraining inflationary pressures, for instance, those explicated here in a later chapter.

ADVICE TO THE EU

First and foremost: it is a shame that in the late 1990s and early 2000s conservative, restrictive economic policies and policymakers are still dominant in many countries and in several international bodies, such as the IMF, the World Bank, the WTO, and also the European Union. These countries and supra-national bodies are still relying on obsolete monetarist and ultra-monetarist, namely New Classical, dogmas, when the very theoretical basis of these doctrines, the strictly exogenous character of the money supply, has ceased to exist in reality in important industrialized countries. For instance, in the United States the money supply became in effect endogenous after 1987.

It is deeply anachronistic that while, according to Krugman (1994:120), the Clinton administration did apply Keynesian measures with "tax incentives for investment" and "a number of public work projects" to boost the economy in 1993, and already then "Keynesianism was not only back, it was almost unchallenged" (ibid., p. 219), and while, according to Jones (1994:91 and 99), the Fed in the United States works on the basis of "neo-Wicksellian theory" and "a modified Keynesian aggregate demand model", and finally provides a basically Post Keynesian, endogenous money supply, in the European Union both leading economists and politicians still live or pretend to live in a monetarist dream-world. Prominent Social Democratic leaders in the United Kingdom and above all in Germany still subscribe to monetarist austerity programs and budget restrictions at a time when the main problem in most countries on the European continent is high unemployment.

It is high time to replace the monetarist or New Classical economic experts and policymakers in the international bodies mentioned, particularly in the European Union, and above all within the hidebound, even petrified Brussels bureaucracy.

The fact that by today the money supply has been made essentially endogenous by the central banks in important countries means that Keynesian aggregate demand management can be financed by monetization rather than either by taxes or by bonds. In consequence, recent worries like those expressed, for instance, by Esping-Andersen (1996c:256), saying that "(g)overnments' freedom to conduct fiscal and monetary policy 'at will' is therefore more constrained: profligate deficit spending to maintain employment or pursue redistributive ambitions will be punished; Keynesianism, let alone social democracy, in one country is accordingly no more an option", have become somewhat exaggerated. One should rather listen to the words of Edin and Carlsson (1995:25), who encourage "not being paralysed by the budget deficit and, as is done so often, insisting that every measure must be 'financed'". As they add: "A fully financed measure intended to benefit a group or industry in the labour market in practice leads only to a redistribution of unemployment" (ibid.).

Indeed, to perceive the public sector economy as a zero-sum game within the strict delimitations of a nonmonetized governmental budget is wrong and obsolete. By means of a monetized compound Keynesian expansion (CKE) a government can enlarge public sector activities together with the size of the whole economy of a country without fear. A properly monetized CKE may yield balanced, proportional growth without inflationary effects.

In order to decrease the rather high level of unemployment in the European Union there is no need to imitate recent policies in the United States (and also the United Kingdom) aiming at the deregulation of labour laws, weakening of trade unions and the subsequent worsening of social inequality (cf. Johansson 1998). Europe should choose more progressive ways. If it comes to following American policies, not these wrong examples should be followed but the good, for instance, the Employment Act of 1946, which, according to Galbraith and Darity (1994:300), "declared that the economic goals of the nation were to achieve 'maximum employment, production and purchasing power'". In 1978 "the wording of the employment objective" was changed by Congress "from 'maximum employment' to 'full employment'", Galbraith and Darity (ibid.) add. In the EU it is high time to modify the Maastricht Treaty and its follow-up pacts, for instance, the Amsterdam Treaty and the Stability and Growth Pact, in ways of giving more emphasis to genuine full employment as the supreme goal of economic policy.

As mentioned by Sollenius (1996:47), the EMU, the Economic and Monetary Union (this is the exact, correct name), within the European Union should only be completely introduced on condition that beforehand or simultaneously an effective system for fighting unemployment in every member country is established. The final stage in the whole system of EMU, the introduction of tangible currency, even together with the earlier enacted Phase Two, should be postponed either until each member country has cured its own unemployment (possibly using some of the ideas suggested above, for instance, each country monetizing its own compound Keynesian expansion, if necessary) or until an effective common system for fighting unemployment is established. Sweden could and should take the initiative by proposing a transformation of the Maastricht Treaty, together with its recent supplements: the Amsterdam Treaty and the Stability and Growth Pact, in a Keynesian direction (about the drawbacks of the Maastricht system, cf. Johansson 1994a:269-270, and Memorandum 1998:6-7).

In other words, a total review of all existing rules should take place before 1 January 2002, the entrance day of the tangible Euro, or else this date should be postponed.

In particular the rules about the European Central Bank, ECB, should be changed so that it can behave in a more sensitive way towards the problem of unemployment. The prevalent reign of the rich man's economics, the strict priority of price stability, of fighting inflation, should be ended and the right weight should be given to the goal of curing unemployment. The money supply can and should be made properly endogenous if the central bank in charge behaves in an appropriate way, in other words, if appropriate democratic political influence or control can guide it to do so. Let the Euro be a little 'softer', if that be the cost, but the level of unemployment in the European countries should be reduced below 5 or 4 percent.

Conservative economists in Sweden often recall that a few decades ago the Swedish Crown and Germany's DM were currencies at about parity value. Today the DM is worth about four times more than the Swedish Crown, due to the long periods of higher inflation in Sweden than in Germany, they lament. But these conservative economists never mention that most people in Sweden lived considerably more happily during these decades of very low unemployment levels, while in Germany many more people suffered from actual unemployment or the heavy psychological threat of unemployment, and/or fewer or worse welfare services. For a great part of the population the price of lower inflation and a harder currency was a lower quality of life.

Parallel to the completion of a monetary union, before the final introduction of the tangible common currency, it would be necessary to work out a systematic Common Employment Policy, CEP, also making use of the idea of compound Keynesian expansion and taking into consideration a basically endogenous character of the money supply pending on the proper, reformed behaviour of the European Central Bank. The idea in a nutshell is as follows: since the EMU implies eliminating the possibility of devaluation as a means of creating jobs in one or the other country, any member country having an unemployment rate higher than 4 percent (or 5 percent) should be allowed to apply compound Keynesian expansions monetized by the European Central Bank or the central banks of the member states (these banks together with the ECB form the European System of Central Banks), until its public finances and its unemployment are cured. (For that matter, the European Central Bank itself and the European System of Central Banks as a whole should be placed under the democratic political control of the European people, possibly via the European Parliament, in addition to the national parliaments.) In other words, a common fund (cf. the "stability fund" in Andersson et al. 1996:15, and Modigliani et al.

1998:12 about the European Structural Funds) with an international European management, financed by the ECB or the whole ESCB, should be set up for the purpose of monetizing compound public sector expansions in those countries or possibly even regions where the rate of unemployment is higher than an agreed normative level, say, 4 or 5 percent (the amounts of support could be comparable to those within the present Common Agricultural Policy, for Sweden cf. Johansson 1994b:12-13).

RESTRAINING INFLATION

INCOMES AGREEMENTS

The choice of priority between fighting unemployment and fighting inflation is not merely a question of economics but a main ideological and political question in our times. A well-known argument in the debate is the following: unemployment only affects an unfortunate minority of the whole population, while inflation affects everyone, hence it is more important to fight inflation. However, the fear of unemployment may often afflict the vast majority of the population, nearly everyone, so unemployment is usually the most important economic plague to cure. Besides that, a constant level of moderate, low inflation is quite tolerable for the majority of the population.

Nevertheless, in favour of fighting inflation there is a somewhat less frequently mentioned cross-frontline argument, namely the fact that high inflation contributes to an increase in unemployment. The reason is the fact, mentioned earlier, that Keynes's (1936:135-146, especially 140-141) "marginal efficiency of capital", that is to say, the expected rate of profit on productive investments, has to "exceed" the "current rate of interest" or the "market rate of interest" (ibid., pp. 136-137); in effect today the expected rate of profit has to be greater than the nominal rate of interest on possible rival financial investments in order to motivate investors to choose the productive alternative. It is not the real but the nominal interest that any productive investment alternative has to compete with in order to be worthwhile, and the higher the inflation rate the higher the nominal interest rate, because the latter is the real interest rate plus the rate of inflation, as we know after Fisher (1907). Thus the higher the inflation rate the higher the nominal interest rate, the more difficult to gain an even higher profit from a would-be productive investment, hence the fewer the productive investments and in consequence the higher the unemployment.

This is in fact a very simple, logical, but comparatively rarely used explanation of the phenomenon of "stagflation". Thus high inflation should be fought, decreased, and, if possible, prevented, even instrumentally, that is to say, in order to decrease or prevent unemployment, the main, more significant economic evil.

If the money supply in a country proves to be endogenous, it by no means implies that there can be no inflationary pressure in the economy at all. Endogenous money supply only means that the money supply by and large accomodates to money demand, and hence also to the money demand caused by increases in output. For example, it can accomodate to an increase in output caused by a governmental action, a compound Keynesian expansion financed by monetization. Then the government should not worry about whether the monetization leads to inflation, because the money supply, not least through the regulatory activities of the central bank to keep the interest rate fixed at an optimum level, will flexibly and suitably accomodate the real needs of the economy corresponding to the new, increased level of output.

So far so good. But some additional, inflationary money demand may come from particularistic, egoistic individual and group-interests, and it is easy to see that the likelihood of this can be comparatively high even in balanced and healthy economies. The well-known two main types of such inflationary pressure are the wage-cost-push and the demand-pull types of inflation. The first type mainly originates in the desire of some occupational groups to gain higher remuneration compared to other groups, and the second in the general desire of enterprises to gain higher profits by raising prices when selling goes well.

Now we do not tackle a third type: the case of the so-called "shortage" inflation, when the basis of inflation is the real shortage of goods compared to the natural demand for them. Such sad situations may occur after wars, natural disasters, etc.; furthermore, unfortunately, they may occur even in peacetime in the less developed countries of the world, wherever the low level of production cannot yet satisfy normal demand.

It is important to realize that the main culprit in generating inflation in modern, industrialized countries is not the government and not the public sector. A democraticly elected government and all democraticly elected local administrations, at least in theory, work for the public good, act in the common interest of the people. The root of inflationary pressure lies hidden in individual and group-egoism, the very driving force of market economy, for that matter.

Since in our contemporary advanced, industrialized societies people are to a great extent still motivated to work by economic incentives (see Sollenius 1983:78-82, 186), inflationary pressure in fact originates automatically, so to say, in the 'normal driving greed' of contemporary society. Trade unions may fight for particularistic group-interests and press for higher wage-rises than others get, and private enterprises, both producers and traders, raise prices in their individual and group interests whenever they think they can do so without a drop in sales.

In hard times, during periods of recession, the fear of unemployment prevents excessive wage demands and the slump in sales prevents demand-pull inflation, but what about the good times? If, as it is hoped, a "Modern Keynesian" trend of economic policies, not least by means of Combined Keynesian Expansions, successfully mitigates recessions and cures unemployment, then how can inflation be bridled effectively? Will inflation not soar up? Will the whole burden of restraining inflation be put exclusively on the shoulders of the central bank, which can then try to "fine-tune" interest rates upwards, as the Fed does from time to time in our days? Not exclusively.

Both wage-cost-push and demand-pull inflation can be analysed with the help of the well-known rule of the "Prisoners' Dilemma". All participants in the economic game try to press for higher prices in exchange for their own work or their own products separately, but for lack of co-ordination they all may end up worse off, because the aggregate result may be high inflation for all, decreasing the real value of their remuneration and wiping out their individual or group gains.

The best solution to the problem of both wage-cost-push and demand-pull inflation thus lies hidden in the principle of co-ordination, which may be embodied in practical arrangements under the often belittled, good old expression: incomes policy. According to Galbraith and Darity (1994:402), also the "post-Keynesians advocate a variety of policy interventions, known as incomes policies, that serve the purpose of influencing and coordinating the expectations of economic agents". However, since the meaning of the phrase "incomes policy" might still be mistaken for some kinds of incomes controls, something which is forced on the participants from above, we have to emphasize that incomes policy should always be placed as much as possible on the basis of negotiated agreements. As regards the question of incomes controls or "wage-price controls" as such, a thorough debate is presented, for instance, by Gill (1976:173-227), and a brief overview of "the theory and history" of incomes policies used in various countries in recent decades is given by Galbraith and Darity (1994:469-481).

Some versions of administrative wage and price controls are used from time to time for anti-inflationary purposes, but they are often regarded as an imperfect method. One partly justified point of criticism blames them for their non-differentiating character. In other words, if applied for too long they are supposed to hinder the important informative and selective functions of the spontaneous, free formation of prices in the economy. But wage-price controls forced on the participants from above, which they may want to shirk, are much less effective than a system of convincing people, of obtaining their agreement, their co-operation. For this reason it is perhaps even better if we speak of "incomes agreements", possibly as parts of still wider "social pacts" or "social contracts", and not merely about incomes policy.

Such a system of incomes agreements should create nation-wide consensus on the question of the tolerable and permittable degree of inflation in a country, with the help of thorough debates and wide, open media coverage. The debates could be started at a high level, by the experts of the government. As Okun (1975, reprinted in Mankiw and Romer 1991c:370) says in a section entitled "Incomes policy": "a case for price-wage intervention by the government emerges ..., the government can be constructive by promoting a noninflationary criterion (or "guidepost")". Heap (1992:152) also says that "centralized wage and price-setting institutions are better placed than decentralized ones to select the equilibrium".

The two main pillars of accomplishing and also putting into practice a desirable consensus could be: the system of centralized, co-ordinated wage-talks to restrain wage-cost-push inflation on the one hand, and the system of voluntary but organized consumer boycotts to restrain demand-pull inflation on the other hand.

Both of these suggested systems may be considered "extra-economic" or "non-economic" by orthodox economists, but in reality there are no demarcation lines, nor should there be any whatsoever between economic, political, sociological and psychological approaches or methods; society is a complicated, complex phenomenon, and all social science disciplines should be intertwined when analysing and influencing it.

The topic of centralized wage-negotiations is a well-known and often debated question, while the idea of consumer boycotts is, as far as I know, a fairly new suggestion. Indeed, the "Swedish model", as it was known for several decades, comprised among other features, a system of centralized wage-negotiations, which worked well as long as these talks were centralized, that is, up to 1982. According to Aberg (1994:80-81), "centralized bargaining prevents wage leapfrogging which was why it developed. In decentralized bargaining, all have an incentive to do better than others ... . This is rational from the individual point of view but the collective outcome is inefficient. Thus, centralized bargaining is supposed to solve a prisoners' dilemma by coordinating individual wage claims and preventing the sum of them from exceeding productivity growth in the whole economy." A similar idea was emphasized also by Dombos (1985).

Crouch (1994:176) writes about the "practice of incomes policy" that "(d)uring the 1960s and 1970s, these policies usually comprised some tripartite arrangement rather than simple state intervention ...". Indeed, the three-way model is the classic and best arrangement of centralized wage-negotiations, with the Government, "Big Business" and "Big Labour" as the participants. Apart from the forgivable irony, this is really the best contemporary model, worth introducing or reintroducing in modern, industrialized countries. The widely used terms "corporate model" and "corporatism" are misleading and are in all likelihood deliberately kept alive and used by conservative social scientists in order to sustain its pejorative terminological and mental association with Mussolini's "corporations". For that matter, the adjective "corporate" and the word "corporation" also have quite another contemporary neutral meaning; today they simply refer to large business organizations in phrases like "corporate capital", "big corporations", etc. (cf. Korten 1995).

Better, more appropriate names for the tripartite system of centralized wage-talks, which system is highly recommendable and should be preserved or renewed everywhere, could be the "co-ordinated model" or the "co-operating model".

According to Crouch (1994:187), "... the inability of the official union level to coordinate lower, and in particular company, levels" was "the ... 'defect' ... that has recently caused such trouble in Scandinavia ...", in other words, this led to the unfortunate dissolution of the system of centralized bargaining. Crouch (ibid., pp.193-194) predicts "considerable intervention by governments to try to stimulate coordination - not by long-term direct government measures as such, but by mechanisms to induce co-operative ... behaviour by reluctant, fragmenting social partners themselves".

Edin (1988:28-29), with the aim of restoring the centralized system of talks in Sweden, looks back on the history of wage-talks and emphasizes the significance of recognizing the antagonist party in the talks as a lasting and also strong counterpart, even sometimes helping the other party to "deliver" to its members (ibid., p. 35). He expresses hopes to include both the employers and the trade unions of the growing service sector in a newly formed model of central negotiations (ibid., p. 36). Edin (1995b:6-7) urges the restoration of the formerly exemplary system of centralized wage negotiations in Sweden in order to restrain wage inflation.

Johansson et al. (1999a) reveal that the faulty contemporary system of wage negotiations in Sweden also contributes to the high unemployment level. Primarily it is the employers' federation that is to be blamed for this, because for obsolete ideological reasons they refuse to take part in centralized talks. Johansson (1998) recalls that a conservative economist, following the fashionable contemporary trend of labour market deregulation, recently even raised the idea of promoting individual wage contracts, as if this were something new. Indeed, this idea is even more retrograde than Mrs. Thatcher's Pharisaic slogan of "free collective bargaining" in the 1980s, which aimed at the fragmentation and weakening of the trade unions - the smaller the better. The idea of individual wage contracts goes only one but a long step further back in time, leading us back to the world of early 19th-century capitalism, into the age before the evolution of the well-organized labour movement, the modern trade unions. It must have been a happy time for employers, no wonder conservative experts propose to bring it back, but it is unfair to pretend that individual wage contracts are a brand new invention. Does the key to our future lie hidden in the last century? Again: a last-century future for us?

CONSUMER BOYCOTTS

While a system of centralized, co-ordinated wage negotiations is needed to restrain wage-cost-push inflation, the new idea of voluntary but organized consumer boycotts is suggested as a means of combating demand-pull inflation. Consumer boycotts could be organized for anti-inflationary purposes selectively, with a differentiating character. They could be initiated on the basis of preliminary investigations by groups of experts into the fairness of price setting with respect to individual products, firms, economic sectors, at any level (cf. the Consumer Council in England, producing their well-known magazine "Which?"). Thus consumer boycotts against unjustified price rises could be organized in highly selective and informative ways. The expert groups could be financed and the boycotts initiated and advertised by trade unions, business associations of honest producers or traders, government agencies, or joint commissions set up by all the three main parties involved: labour, business, and government.

The method of consumer boycotts naturally builds only on the voluntary behaviour and participation of consumers, but in our industrialized societies the mass communication media are very effective, and their powerful influence should be used fully to mobilize the consumers. The media can also be widely used to utilize the process of organizing the boycotts as a means of two-way communications; in other words, the opinion of the consumers should also be gathered and reflected back to the centrally formed expert groups. In this way the organizational channels of the boycotts could also work in the other direction and help to foster a nation-wide debate to form a consensus on general incomes agreements. Both this feed-back communication and the boycotts themselves may well be regarded as manifestations of a kind of "economic democracy".

Concerning a possible theoretical objection to consumer boycotts on the basis that they might decrease consumption too much, the answer is that in modern societies the general trend is overconsumption, anyway. The advanced, industrialized countries devour disproportionally large shares of the world's natural resources, and some moderation of their consumption habits could only be beneficial for Boulding's (1968) and Korten's (1995:25) earlier mentioned "spaceship Earth".

There is some reason to suppose that in most cases people will behave in their role as consumers fairly conscientiously and responsibly. The method is supposed to take effect and exert a restraining influence on prices not only and not even primarily in direct ways, through the number of actually investigated and boycotted inflationary goods and their producers or traders, but also and much more widely in indirect ways, through the general deterrent value of all the well-publicized cases and the whole system of consumer checks, expert groups and potential boycotts. Therefore the method of consumer boycotts might prove to be an effective, and often even preventive anti-inflationary tool in the future.

REFERENCES

Aberg, Rune
   1994   "Wage control and cost-push inflation in Sweden since 1960"
in Dore et al. (1994), Chapter 4, pp. 71-93.

Ahrne, Göran
   1989   <u>Byrakratin och statens inre gränser</u>.
("The bureaucracy and the internal boundaries of the state.")
Stockholm: Rabén & Sjögren.

   1994a   "Organiseringen av det civila samhället"
("The organization of the civil society")
<u>Sociologisk Forskning</u> Vol. 31, No. 2, pp. 38-45.

   1994b   <u>Social Organizations</u>:
Interaction inside, outside and between organizations.
London: Sage Publications.

   1995   "Omvandlingen fran individ till samhälle"
("The transformation from individual to society")
<u>Dansk Sociologi</u> Vol. 6, No. 1, pp. 55-64.

   1997   <u>De ofrivilliga passagerarna</u>.
En analys av staten ur ett organisationsteoretiskt perspektiv
("The involuntary passengers.
An analysis of the state from an organization theoretical perspective")
Stockholm: SCORE
Stockholms centrum för forskning om offentlig sektor

   1998a   "The Organizational Construction of Social Citizenship"
in Flösser and Otto (1998), pp. 165-172.

Ahrne, Göran
  1998b "Stater och andra organisationer"
       ("States and other organizations")
       in Ahrne (1998c), Kapitel (Chapter) 5, pp. 123-156.

  1998c <u>Stater som organisationer</u>. (Ed. by Göran Ahrne)
       ("States as organizations.")
       Stockholm: Nerenius & Santérus Förlag.

Ahrne, Göran and Peter Hedström
  1999 <u>Organisationer och samhälle</u>: Analytiska perspektiv.
      ("Organizations and society: Analytical perspectives.")
      Lund: Studentlitteratur.

Ahrne, Göran and Roine Johansson
  1994 "Between Organizations"
      in Ahrne (1994b), Chapter 6, pp. 114-131.

Ahrne, Göran, Christine Roman and Mats Franzén
  1996 <u>Det sociala landskapet</u>:
      En sociologisk beskrivning av Sverige fran 50-tal till 90-tal
      ("The social landscape: A sociological description of Sweden
      from the 1950s to the 1990s")
      Göteborg:Bokförlaget Korpen.

Andersson, Dan
  1998 <u>Pa väg mot en ny modell</u>:
      Politik mot arbetslöshet och för ökad reallön.
      ("On the way toward a new model:
      Policy against unemployment and for increased real wage.")
      Stockholm: LO Landsorganisationen i Sverige.

Andersson, Dan, Jeanette Envall, Asa-Pia Järliden, Mats Morin and Lena Westerlund
1996 Wage Earners and EMU:
A report by the economists of the
Swedish Trade Union Confederation
Stockholm: LO Landsorganisationen i Sverige.

Baron, James N. and Michael T. Hannan
1994 "The Impact of Economics on Contemporary Sociology"
Journal of Economic Literature
Vol. XXXII, September, pp. 1111-1146.

Baumol, William
1952 "The Transactions Demand for Cash:
An Inventory Theoretic Approach"
Quarterly Journal of Economics November.

Benner, Mats
1997 The Politics of Growth:
Economic Regulation in Sweden 1930-1994.
Lund: Arkiv Förlag.

1998 "Välfärdskapitalismens era" ("The era of welfare capitalism")
in Elmlund and Glans (1998), pp. 129-143.

Berglund, Per Gunnar
1996 Konsten att avskaffa arbetslösheten.
("The art of eliminating unemployment.")
Stockholm: Ordfronts förlag.

Bernanke, Ben S. and Alan S. Blinder
1988 "Credit, Money, and Aggregate Demand"
American Economic Review Vol. 78 (May) pp. 435-439.

Blix, Erik
  1999   "All världens hopp star till Internet"
         Metro February 22, Monday, p. 6.

Bottomore, Tom
  1985   Theories of Modern Capitalism.
         London: George Allen & Unwin.

Boulding, Kenneth
  1968   "The Economics of the Coming Spaceship Earth"
         in Jarrett (1968), pp. 3-14.

Boyer, Robert
  1990   The Regulation School: A Critical Introduction.
         Translated by Craig Charney.
         New York: Columbia University Press.

Bradley, Philip D. (Ed.)
  1959   The Public Stake in Union Power.
         University of Virginia Press.

Brown, A. J.
  1955   The Great Inflation, 1939-1951.
         London: Oxford University Press.

Brunner, Karl and Allan H. Meltzer (Eds.)
  1976   Policies for Employment, Prices, and Exchange Rates.
         Vol. 11 of Carnegie-Rochester Series on Public Policy.
         Amsterdam: North-Holland Publishing Company.

Bryant, John
  1983   "A Simple Rational-Expectations Keynes-Type Model"
         Quarterly Journal of Economics Vol. 98 (August) pp. 525-528.

Buiter, W. H.
   1980 "The Macroeconomics of Dr Pangloss:
          A Critical Survey of the New Classical Macroeconomics"
          Economic Journal.

Chancellor, Edward
   1999 Devil Take the Hindmost:
          A History of Financial Speculation.
          London, Basingstoke: Macmillan.

Clower, R. W.
   1965 "The Keynesian Counter-revolution: A Theroretical Appraisal"
          in Hahn and Brechling (1965), Chapter 5.

   1969 Monetary Theory. (Ed. by R. W. Clower)
          Harmondsworth: Penguin

Colander, David C. and Dewey Daane (Eds.)
   1994 The Art of Monetary Policy.
          Armonk, New York - London, England: M. E. Sharpe.

Cooper, Russell and Andrew John
   1988 "Coordinating Coordination Failures in Keynesian Models"
          Quarterly Journal of Economics Vol. 103 (August) pp. 441-463.

Council of Economic Advisers
   1996 Job Creation and Employment Opportunities:
          The United States Labor Market, 1993-1996.
          A Report by the Council of Economic Advisers with the
          U.S. Department of Labor, Office of the Chief Economist.
          April 23, 1996.

Coy, Peter
   1997 "Headed for Bubble Trouble?
          The market rebound may be investor optimism run amok"
          Business Week November 17, pp. 66-67.

Crouch, Colin
   1993   <u>Industrial Relations and European State Traditions</u>.
           Oxford: Clarendon Press.

   1994   "Incomes policies, institutions and markets:
           an overview of recent developments"
           in Dore et al. (1994), Chapter 9, pp. 175-196.

Daane, Dewey
   1994   "The Federal Open Market Committee in Action" in
           Colander and Daane (1994), Chapter 11, pp. 135-146.

Dombos, Paul
   1979   "Some Recent Changes in the Swedish Occupational Structure"
           <u>Acta Sociologica</u> Vol. 22, No. 4, pp. 321-343.

   1985   "Den gyllene medelvägen"
           ("The golden mean")
           <u>Aftonbladet</u> November 21, p. 2.

Dore, Ronald, Robert Boyer and Zoe Mars (Eds.)
   1994   <u>The Return to Incomes Policy</u>.
           London - New York: Pinter Publishers

Dornbusch, Rudiger and Stanley Fischer
   1990   <u>Macroeconomics</u>. Fifth Edition.
           New York: McGraw-Hill.

   1994   <u>Macroeconomics</u>. Sixth Edition.
           New York: McGraw-Hill.

Dornbusch, Rudiger, Stanley Fischer and Richard Startz
   1998   <u>Macroeconomics</u>. Seventh Edition.
           New York: McGraw-Hill.

Edin, Per-Olof
   1988 "Förnuftets väg eller den svenska modellen"
         ("Reason's way or the Swedish model")
         in Edin et al. (1988) pp. 25-36.

   1995a <u>Fifty-nine Points for Increased Economic Growth</u>
         LO and the LO affiliates' joint programme for increased
         growth in the Swedish economy. September 1995.
         Stockholm: LO Swedish Trade Union Confederation.

   1995b <u>Three Ways To Fight Inflation</u>
         (of which two can lead to full employment)
         Stockholm: LO Swedish Trade Union Confederation.

Edin, Per-Olof and Dan Andersson
   1995 <u>Seven Myths about Sweden's Economic Crisis</u>
         Stockholm: LO Swedish Trade Union Confederation.

Edin, Per-Olof and Stig Carlsson
   1995 <u>Sweden can afford it!</u>
         The LO economists explain the economic crisis
         in everyday language.
         Stockholm: LO The Swedish Trade Union Confederation

Edin, Per-Olof, Olle Hammarström, Bengt K A Johansson, Allan Larsson
      and Björn Rosengren
   1988 <u>Mot en ny svensk modell</u>
         Stockholm: Tidens förlag.

Editorial
   1997a "Lesson One: Asian hubris is blinding its leaders."
         <u>Business Week</u> November 10, p. 116.

Editorial
   1997b "Asia: End Crony Capitalism"
         <u>Business Week</u> November 17, p. 98.

Ehrenberg, Johan
  1995 Pengar, Makt & Alla Vi Andra. Tredje upplagan.
        ("Money, power and all we others. Third edition.")
        ETC-bok.

  1996 Mera Pengar. ("More money.")
        Stockholm: Norstedts Förlag.

Ekdahl, Ake
  1999 "Smockor med forskartyngd" ("Wits with scholarly weight")
        Dagens Nyheter January 20, Wednesday, p. B 5.

Elmlund, Peter and Kay Glans (Eds.)
  1998 Den välsignade tillväxten: tankelinjer kring ett
        arhundrade av kapitalism, teknik, kultur och vetenskap.
        ("The blessed growth: lines of thought around a century of
        capitalism, technology, culture and science.")
        Stockholm: Natur och Kultur.

Elster, Jon
  1979 Ulysses and the Sirens.
        New York: Cambridge University Press.

  1986 Karl Marx: A Reader. (Ed. by Jon Elster)
        Cambridge: Cambridge University Press.

Erikson, Robert
  1992 "Social policy and inequality in health:
        Considerations from the Swedish experience"
        International Journal of Health Sciences
        Vol. 3, No. 3/4 (September/December) pp. 215-222.

Erikson, Robert and John H. Goldthorpe
  1992 The Constant Flux:
        A Study of Class Mobility in Industrial Societies.
        Oxford: Clarendon Press.

Erikson, Robert and Jan O. Jonsson
- 1996a "Explaining Class Inequality in Education:
  The Swedish Test Case"
  in Erikson and Jonsson (1996c), Introduction, pp. 1-63.

- 1996b "The Swedish Context: Educational Reform
  and Long-term Change in Educational Inequality"
  in Erikson and Jonsson (1996c), Chapter 1, pp. 65-93.

- 1996c Can Education Be Equalized?
  The Swedish Case in Comparative Perspective.
  Boulder, Colorado: Westview Press.

Erikson, Robert, Erik Jörgen Hansen, Stein Ringen and Hannu Uusitalo (Eds.)
- 1987 The Scandinavian Model:
  Welfare States and Welfare Research.
  Armonk, New York: M. E. Sharpe, Inc.

Esping-Andersen, Gösta
- 1990 The Three Worlds of Welfare Capitalism.
  Princeton: Princeton University Press.

- 1996a "After the Golden Age?
  Welfare State Dilemmas in a Global Economy"
  in Esping-Andersen (1996d), Chapter 1, pp. 1-31.

- 1996b "Welfare States without Work: the Impasse of Labour Shedding
  and Familialism in Continental European Social Policy"
  in Esping-Andersen (1996d), Chapter 3, pp. 66-87.

- 1996c "Positive-Sum Solutions in a World of Trade-Offs?"
  in Esping-Andersen (1996d) Chapter 9: Conclusion, pp. 256-267

Esping-Andersen, Gösta
  1996d <u>Welfare States in Transition</u>:
       National Adaptations in Global Economies.
       (Ed. by Gösta Esping-Andersen)
       London: Sage Publications.

  1999   <u>Social Foundations of Postindustrial Economies</u>.
       Oxford: Oxford University Press.

Etzioni, Amitai
  1988   <u>The Moral Dimension: Toward a New Economics</u>.
       New York: The Free Press.

Evans, Peter B., Dietrich Rueschemeyer and Theda Skocpol (Eds.)
  1985   <u>Bringing the State Back In</u>.
       Cambridge: Cambridge University Press.

Fellner, William
  1959   "Demand Inflation, Cost Inflation, and Collective Bargaining"
       in Bradley (1959).

Fischer, Stanley (Ed.)
  1980   <u>Rational Expectations and Economic Policy</u>.
       Chicago: The University of Chicago Press.

Fisher, Irving
  1907   <u>The Rate of Interest</u>. New York: Macmillan

  1926   "A Statistical Relation Between Unemployment
       and Price Changes"
       <u>International Labour Review</u>
       Reprinted in Journal of Political Economy
       1973., March/April, pp. 496-502.

  1930   <u>Theory of Interest</u>. New York: Macmillan.

Flösser, Gaby and Hans-Uwe Otto (Eds.)
1998 Towards More Democracy in Social Services.
Walter de Gruyter.

Friedman, Benjamin M.
1979 "Optimal Expectations and the Extreme Information Assumptions of 'Rational Expectations' Macromodels"
Journal of Monetary Economics

Friedman, Benjamin M. and Lawrence H. Summers
1991 "Series Foreword" in Mankiw and Romer (1991c), pp. ix-x.

Friedman, Milton
1966 "Comments" in Shultz and Aliber (1966), pp. 55-61.

1968 "The Role of Monetary Policy"
American Economic Review Vol. 58, No. 1 (March) pp. 1-17.

1973 "The Key Propositions of Monetarism" in Friedman, Milton
Money and Economic Development:The Horowitz Lectures of 1972.
New York: Praeger Publishers, Inc.

Fukuyama, Francis
1989 "The End of History?"
The National Interest No. 16 (Summer) pp. 3-18.

1990 "Are We at the End of History?"
Fortune No. 2 (January 15) pp. 33-36.

Furaker, Bengt
1987 Stat och offentlig sektor.
("State and public sector.")
Stockholm: Rabén & Sjögren.

Galbraith, James K. and William Darity, Jr.
1994 Macroeconomics. Boston: Houghton Mifflin Company.

Galbraith, John Kenneth
   1967   The New Industrial State.
         Boston: Houghton Mifflin.

Gill, Richard T.
   1976   Great Debates in Economics. Volume II: Analysis and Policy.
         Pacific Palisades, California: Goodyear Publishing Company.

Godley, Wynne
   1999   "The US economy: An impossible balancing act"
         Finacial Times Personal view, February 19, Friday, p. 14.

Gran, Brian K.
   1997   "Book Reviews"
         Acta Sociologica Vol. 40, No. 3, pp. 304-308.

Granovetter, Mark
   1985a Roundtable on the 'New Sociology of Economic Life'
         ASA Meetings, Washington, DC. Unpublished outline.

   1985b "Economic Action and Social Structure:
         The Problem of Embeddedness"
         American Journal of Sociology
         Vol. 91, No. 3 (November) pp. 481-510.

   1990   Interview by Richard Swedberg.
         In Swedberg (1990), Chapter 5, pp. 96-114.

Granovetter, Mark and Richard Swedberg (Eds.)
   1992   The Sociology of Economic Life
         Boulder, Colorado: Westview Press.

Gregory, Paul R. and Roy J. Ruffin
   1994   Macroeconomics. New York: HarperCollins.

Greider, Göran
1995 "Lyssna inte när pengarna pratar politik:
De senaste artiondena har den nationalekonomiska vetenskapen
blivit ideologi"
("Do not listen when money speaks politics:
In the latest decades economic science
has become ideology")
Dagens Nyheter November 1, p. B 3.

Gustafsson, Rolf A
1995 "Recensioner: Hugemark, Agneta (1994)
Den fängslande marknaden.
Ekonomiska experter om välfärdsstaten."
("Recensions: Hugemark, Agneta, 1994, The imprisoning market.
Economic experts about the welfare state.")
Sociologisk Forskning Vol. 32, No. 4, pp. 92-98.

Hahn, F. H. and F. Brechling (Eds.)
1965 The Theory of Interest Rates. Basingstoke: Macmillan.

Hall, Robert E. and N. Gregory Mankiw
1994 "Nominal Income Targeting"
in Mankiw (1994), Chapter 2, pp. 71-93.

Halmos, Paul
1970 Personal Service Society.
London: Constable.

Hansen, Alvin
1949 Monetary Theory and Fiscal Policy. New York: McGraw-Hill.

Heap, Shaun P. Hargreaves
1992 The New Keynesian Macroeconomics:
Time, Belief and Social Interdependence.
Aldershot, England: Edward Elgar Publishing Ltd.

Hedström, Peter
   1998   "Rational imitation"
           in Hedström and Swedberg (1998b), Chapter 12, pp. 306-327.

Hedström, Peter and Richard Swedberg
   1996   "Rational Choice, Empirical Research,
           and the Sociological Tradition"
           European Sociological Review Vol. 12, No. 2, pp. 127-146.

   1998a   "Social mechanisms: An introductory essay"
           in Hedström and Swedberg (1998b), Chapter 1, pp. 1-31.

   1998b   Social Mechanisms:
           An Analytical Approach to Social Theory.
           (Edited by Peter Hedström and Richard Swedberg)
           Cambridge: Cambridge University Press.

Hedström, Peter, Richard Swedberg and Lars Udéhn
   1998   "Popper's Situational Analysis and Contemporary Sociology"
           Philosophy of the Social Sciences
           Vol. 28, No. 3 (September) pp. 339-364.

Hicks, John
   1934   "A Review of Myrdal" Economica November.
           Reprinted in Hicks (1982), Chapter 4, pp. 42-45.

   1937   "Mr Keynes and the Classics" Economica April.
           Reprinted in Hicks (1982), Chapter 8, pp. 100-115.

   1977   Economic Perspectives:
           Further Essays on Money and Growth.
           Oxford: Clarendon Press (Oxford University Press).

   1979   "The Formation of an Economist"
           Quarterly Review Banca Nazionale del Lavoro, September.
           Reprinted in Hicks (1984), Chapter 15, pp. 281-290.

Hicks, John
   1982   Money, Interest and Wages.
           Collected Essays on Economic Theory, Volume II.
           Oxford: Basil Blackwell.

   1984   The Economics of John Hicks.
           Selected and with an introduction by Dieter Helm.
           Oxford: Basil Blackwell.

Hillier, Brian
   1991   The Macroeconomic Debate:
           Models of the Closed and Open Economy.
           Oxford: Basil Blackwell.

Hobsbawm, Eric
   1996   Age of Extremes:
           The Short Twentieth Century 1914-1991.
           First published in 1994. This edition by Abacus, 1995.
           Second reprint 1996.
           London: Abacus (A Division of Little, Brown and Company).

   1997   On History. London: Weidenfeld & Nicolson.

Howitt, Peter
   1990   The Keynesian Recovery: And Other Essays.
           Hemel Hempstead, England: Philip Allan.

Hume, David
   1752a "On Money". Reprinted in Hume (1970).

   1752b "On Interest". Reprinted in Hume (1970).

   1970   Writings on Economics. Ed. by Eugene Rotwein.
           Madison: University of Wisconsin Press.

Ingham, Geoffrey
- 1996 "Money is a Social Relation"
  Review of Social Economy Vol. 54, pp. 507-529.

- 1998 "On the Underdevelopment of the 'Sociology of Money'"
  Acta Sociologica Vol. 41, No. 1, pp. 3-18.

Ip, Greg
- 1999 "What's Sparking the Irrepressible Dow? It's the Economy"
  The Wall Street Journal Europe Tuesday, March 30, p. 15.

Jacobsson, B. (Ed.)
- 1994 Organisationsexperiment i kommuner och landsting
  ("Experiments of organization
  in municipalities and counties").
  Stockholm: Nerenius & Santérus.

Jacobsson, Magnus A
- 2000 "Tva miljoner sitter i amerikanska fängelser"
  ("Two millions sit in American prisons")
  Metro Tuesday, February 22, p. 13.

Jarrett, Henry
- 1968 Environmental Quality in a Growing Economy.
  Baltimore: John Hopkins University Press.

Jessop, Bob
- 1990 State Theory: Putting Capitalist States in Their Place.
  Cambridge: Polity Press.

Johansson, Sten
  1994a "Alternativ till medlemskap i EU -
och deras konsekvenser för demokratin"
("Alternatives to membership in EU -
and their consequences for democracy")
<u>Suveränitet och demokrati</u> ("Sovereignty and democracy")
Bilagedel med expertuppsatser till betänkande av
EG-konsekvensutredningarna: Subsidiaritet.
("Enclosed volume with expert studies to the investigations
of EU-consequences: Subsidization.")
Stockholm: Utrikesdepartementet
("The Ministry of Foreign Affairs")
SOU, Statens Offentliga Utredningar
("Official investigations of the state") 1994:12, pp. 235-280

  1994b <u>Vad kostar medlemskapet?</u> ("What does membership cost?")
En kritisk granskning av regeringens uppgifter
("A critical examination of the government's data")
Stockholm: Socialdemokrater mot EU
("Social Democrats against EU")

  1997 "Sverige förnedras i EU" ("Sweden is humiliated in the EU")
<u>Dagens Nyheter</u> DN Debatt, January 20, p. A 4.

  1998 "Ge alla rabatt pa marginalskatten"
("Give all reduction on the marginal tax")
<u>Dagens Nyheter</u> DN Debatt, February 28, p. A 4.

Johansson, Sten and Sören Wibe
  1998 "Farligt öka Riksbankens oberoende"
("Dangerous to increase the Central Bank's independence")
<u>Dagens Nyheter</u> DN Debatt, November 11, p. A 4.

Johansson, Sten, Per Lundborg and Johnny Zetterberg
1999a "Visst är löneökningarna för höga"
("Sure, the wage rises are too high")
Dagens Nyheter DN Debatt, February 18, p. A 4.

1999b Massarbetslöshetens karaktär
och vägarna till full sysselsättning.
Andra reviderade upplagan.
("The character of mass unemployment
and the ways to full employment. Second, revised edition.")
Stockholm: FIEF, Stiftelsen Fackföreningsrörelsens Institut
för Ekonomisk Forskning
("Trade Union Institute for Economic Research").

Jones, David M.
1994 "Monetary Policy as Viewed by a Money Market Participant"
in Colander and Daane (1994), Chapter 7, pp. 85-100.

Kaldor, Nicholas
1970 "The New Monetarism" Lloyd's Bank Review July, pp. 1-17.

1980 Origins of the New Monetarism.
Cardiff: University College Cardiff Press.

1982 The Scourge of Monetarism.
London: Oxford University Press.

Kaldor, Nicholas and James Trevithick
1981 "A Keynesian Perspective on Money"
Lloyd's Bank Review January.

Källberg, Jan
2000 "Vem anställer när IT friställer" ("Who hires when IT fires")
Metro Thursday, March 2, Nytt Job p. 1.

Kalleberg, Arne L.
  1995 "Sociology and Economics: Crossing the Boundaries"
        Social Forces Vol. 73, No. 4 (June) pp. 1207-1218.

Karlsson, Nils (Ed.)
  1996 Sveriges framtida socialförsäkringssystem
        ("Sweden's future social security system")
        City University Press.

Katona, George
  1975 Psychological Economics. New York: Elsevier.

Kerr, Clark
  1983 The Future of Industrial Societies:
        Convergence or Continuing Diversity?
        Cambridge, Massachusetts: Harvard University Press.

Kerr, Clark, John T. Dunlop, Frederick H. Harbison, Charles A. Myers
  1960 Industrialism and Industrial Man:
        The Problem of Labor and Management in Economic Growth.
        Cambridge, Massachusetts: Harvard University Press.

Keynes, John Maynard
  1936 The General Theory of Employment Interest and Money.
        London: Macmillan.

  1937 "The General Theory of Employment"
        Quarterly Journal of Economics
        Vol. 51, February, pp. 209-223.

Kitschelt, Herbert and Staf Hellemans
  1990 Beyond the European Left:
        Ideology and Political Action in the Belgian Ecology Parties.
        Durham and London: Duke University Press.

Kitschelt, Herbert et al. (Eds.)
1997   Continuity and Change in Contemporary Capitalism.
        Cambridge: Cambridge University Press.

Korpi, Walter
1978   The Working Class in Welfare Capitalism:
        Work, Unions and Politics in Sweden.
        London: Routledge and Kegan Paul.

1982   "The Historical Compromise and Its Dissolution"
        in Rydén and Bergström (1982), Chapter 9, pp. 124-141.

1983   The Democratic Class Struggle.
        London: Routledge and Kegan Paul

1987a   "Blott Sverige svensk välfärd äger?
        Välfärdspolitikens drivkrafter och utfall."
        ("Merely Sweden has Swedish welfare?
        The driving forces and results of welfare policy.")
        EInternationella Studier ("International Studies") No. 5.
        Stockholm: Utrikespolitiska Institutet
        ("The Foreign Policy Institute").

1987b   "Maktens isberg under ytan"
        in Petersson (1987), pp. 83-117.
        Stockholm: Carlssons Bokförlag.

1990   The Development of the Swedish Welfare State
        in a Comparative Perspective.
        Stockholm: The Swedish Institute.

1991   "Political and Economic Explanations for Unemployment:
        A Cross-National and Long-Term Analysis"
        British Journal of Political Science
        Vol. 21, Part 3, July, pp. 315-348.

Korpi, Walter
- 1992 Halkar Sverige efter?
Sveriges ekonomiska tillväxt 1820-1990 i jämförande belysning. ("Is Sweden trailing? Sweden's economic growth 1820-1990 in a comparative light.")
Stockholm: Carlsson Bokförlag.

- 1996a "Eurosclerosis and the Sclerosis of Objectivity: On the Role of Values Among Economic Policy Experts" The Economic Journal Vol. 106, pp. 1727-1746.

- 1996b "Ar det svenska socialförsäkringssystemet langsiktigt ohallbart?"
("Is the Swedish social security system untenable in the long run?")
in Karlsson (1996), pp. 120-146.

Korpi, Walter and Joakim Palme
- 1993 "Socialpolitik, kris och reformer: Sverige i internationell belysning"
("Social policy, crisis and reforms: Sweden in international light")
Nya villkor för ekonomi och politik,
rapport till betänkande av Ekonomikommissionen, Bilagedel 2.
("New conditions for economy and politics, report to the deliberations of the Economic Committee, Enclosures, Part 2.")
Stockholm: Finansdepartementet
("The Ministry of Finance")
SOU, Statens Offentliga Utredningar
("Official investigations of the state") 1993:16, pp. 135-170

- 1998 "The Paradox of Redistribution and Strategies of Equality: Welfare State Institutions, Inequality, and Poverty in the Western Countries"
American Sociological Review Vol. 63, pp. 661-687.

Korten, David C.
  1995 When Corporations Rule the World. (Reprinted in 1996)
        London: Earthscan Publications Ltd.

Krugman, Paul
  1994 Peddling Prosperity: Economic Sense and Nonsense
        in the Age of Diminished Expectations.
        New York - London: W.W. Norton & Company.

Leijonhufvud, A.
  1967 "Keynes and the Keynesians: A Suggested Interpretation"
        American Economic Review.

  1968 On Keynesian Economics and the Economics of Keynes:
        A Study in Monetary Theory.
        New York: Oxford University Press.

Leonard, Eugene A.
  1994 "A Monetarist's Confession" in
        Colander and Daane (1994), Chapter 8, pp. 101-105.

Lignell, Anders
  2000a "Sverige bäst i världen pa IT"
        ("Sweden best in the world at IT")
        Metro Thursday, February 17, p. 10.

  2000b "E-post ökar stressen pa jobbet"
        ("E-mail increases stress at job")
        Metro Saturday, February 26, p. 8.

Lucas, Robert E., Jr.
  1969 "Real Wages, Employment, and Inflation"
        Journal of Political Economy
        Vol. 77 (September/October) pp. 721-754.

Lucas, Robert E., Jr.
- 1972 "Expectations and the Neutrality of Money"
Journal of Economic Theory Vol. 4 (April) pp. 103-124.

- 1974 "Equilibrium Search and Unemployment"
Journal of Economic Theory Vol. 7 (February) pp. 188-209.

- 1976 "A Review: Paul McCracken et al.,
Towards Full Employment and Price Stability,
A Report to the OECD by a Group of Independent Experts.
OECD, June 1977." In Brunner and Meltzer (1976), pp. 161-168.

- 1978 "Unemployment Policy" Amerian Economic Review:
Papers and Proceedings. Vol. 68 (May) pp. 353-357.

- 1980 "Rules, Discretion, and the Role of the Economic Advisor"
in Fischer (1980), pp. 199-210.

- 1981 Studies in Business-Cycle Theory.
Cambridge, Massachusetts: MIT Press.

- 1995 Monetary Neutrality.
The Economy Prize Lecture 1995.
Stockholm: The Nobel Foundation.

Mankiw, N. Gregory
- 1986 "The Allocation of Credit and Financial Collapse"
Quarterly Journal of Economics
Vol. 101 (August) pp. 455-470.

- 1994 Monetary Policy Edited by N. Gregory Mankiw.
Chicago and London: The University of Chicago Press.

Mankiw, N. Gregory and David Romer
- 1991a "Introduction" in Mankiw and Romer (1991b), pp. 1-26.

Mankiw, N. Gregory and David Romer (Eds.)
  1991b New Keynesian Economics Vol. 1:
      Imperfect Competition and Sticky Prices.
      MIT Press Readings in Economics
      edited by Benjamin Friedman and Lawrence Summers.
      Cambridge, Massachusetts - London, England: The MIT Press.

  1991c New Keynesian Economics Vol. 2:
      Coordination Failures and Real Rigidities.
      MIT Press Readings in Economics
      edited by Benjamin Friedman and Lawrence Summers.
      Cambridge, Massachusetts - London, England: The MIT Press.

Marshall, T. H.
  1965 Class, Citizenship and Social Development. New York.

Martin, Hans-Peter and Harald Schumann
  1997 The Global Trap:
      Globalization and the assault on prosperity and democracy.
      London & New York: Zed Books Ltd.

Matthews, Robin
  1991 "Animal spirits" in Meeks (1991b), Chapter 7, pp. 103-125.

Matzner, Egon and Wolfgang Streeck (Eds.)
  1991 Beyond Keynesianism:
      The Socio-Economics of Production and Full Employment.
      Aldershot, England: Edward Elgar.

McMurrin, Sterling M. (Ed.)
  1980 The Tanner Lectures on Human Values Vol. I.
      Salt Lake City - Cambridge:
      University of Utah Press - Cambridge University Press.

Meeks, J. Gay Tulip
  1991a "Keynes on the rationality of decision procedures
         under uncertainty: the investment decision"
         in Meeks (1991b), Chapter 8, pp. 126-160.

  1991b Thoughtful economic man:
         Essays on rationality, moral rules and benevolence.
         Edited by J. Gay Tulip Meeks.
         Cambridge: Cambridge University Press.

Memorandum
  1998   Full Employment, Solidarity and Sustainability in Europe:
         Old Challenges, New Opportunities for Economic Policy.
         European Economists for an Alternative Economic Policy.

Metro
  2000a "Varannan svensk surfade i januari"
         ("Every second Swede surfed in January")
         Metro Thursday, February 17, p. 10.

  2000b "Metrofakta: IT i Sverige" ("Metro facts: IT in Sweden")
         Metro Tuesday, February 29, p. 13.

  2000c "Över fem miljoner mobilabonnemang"
         ("Over five million cell-phone subscriptions")
         Metro Saturday, March 11, p. 1.

Modigliani, Franco, Robert Solow, Assar Lindbeck, Beniamino Moro,
         Dennis Snower, Hans Verner Steinherr, Paolo Sylos Lambini
  1998   Economists' Manifesto on Unemployment in the European Union.
         BNL Quarterly Review No. 206, September.

Moggridge, D. (Ed.)
  1973   The Collected Writings of John Maynard Keynes Vol. XIV.
         Basingstoke: Macmillan.

Moore, Basil
   1979   "The Endogenous Money Stock"
            The Journal of Post Keynesian Economics Fall 1979.

   1981   "The Difficulty of Controlling the Money Stock"
            The Journal of Portfolio Management Summer 1981.

Morgan, Brian
   1978   Monetarists and Keynesians:
            Their Contribution to Monetary Theory.
            London and Basingstoke: Macmillan.

Muth, John
   1961   "Rational Expectations and the Theory of Price Movements"
            Econometrica Vol. 29, pp. 299-306.

Myrdal, Gunnar
   1939   Monetary Equilibrium.

Nielsen, Klaus and Ove K. Pedersen
   1990   From the Mixed Economy to the Negotiated Economy:
            The Scandinavian Countries.
            Copenhagen: Center for Public Organization and Management, Copenhagen Business School.

Nordvall, Michael
   2000   "Thaligt skydd mot e-postreklam"
            ("Holed protection against e-mail advertisements")
            Avisen Saturday, February 26, p. 18.

Nussbaum, Martha and Amartya Sen (Eds.)
   1993   The Quality of Life.
            Oxford: Clarendon Press.

Okun, Arthur M.
1975 "Inflation: Its Mechanics and Welfare Costs"
Brookings Papers on Economic Activity No. 2, pp. 351-390.
Brookings Institution.

Olsson, Hans and Peter Holmgren
1994 "Försörjningsbörda, omfördelning och tidsanvändning
i den svenska ekonomin 1965-1992"
("Maintenance burden, redistribution and the use of time
in the Swedish economy 1965-1992")
in Nettokostnader för transfereringar i Sverige
och nagra andra länder.
("Netto costs for transfers in Sweden
and some other countries") Rapport till ESO ("Report to ESO")
Ds 1994:133. Del II ("Part II") pp. 75-109.
Stockholm: Finansdepartementet ("The Ministry of Finance").

Olsson, Hans and Marie Oberkofler
1994 Nettokostnader för transfereringar i Sverige
och nagra andra länder.
("Netto costs for transfers in Sweden
and some other countries") Rapport till ESO ("Report to ESO")
Ds 1994:133. Del I ("Part I") pp. 7-75.
Stockholm: Finansdepartementet ("The Ministry of Finance").

Patinkin, D.
1982 Anticipations of the General Theory.
Oxford: Basil Blackwell.

Pearl, Arthur and Frank Riessman
1965 New Careers for the Poor.
New York.

Pedersen, Ove K. and Projekt Forhandlingsökonomi
1992 Privat Politik ("Private Politics").
Frederiksberg: Samfundslitteratur.

Persson, Gunnar
- 1980 "Skall sjukvarden privatiseras?"
  ("Should the health care be privatized?")
  Ekonomisk debatt ("Economic debate") No. 4.

Petersson, Olof (Ed.)
- 1987 Maktbegreppet ("The notion of power").
  Stockholm: Carlssons Bokförlag.

Phelps, Edmund S.
- 1967 "Phillips Curves, Expectations of Inflation, and Optimal Unemployment over Time"
  Economica Vol. 34, No. 3 (August) pp. 254-281.

- 1968 "Money-Wage Dynamics and Labor-Market Equilibrium"
  Journal of Political Economy
  Vol. 76, Part II, No. 4 (July/August) pp. 687-711.

- 1971 "The 'Natural Rate' Controversy and Economic Theory"
  in Inflation and the Canadian Experience
  Industrial Relations Centre, Queen's University, Kingston, Ontario.

- 1979a "Introduction" to Part II in Phelps (1979b), pp. 93-95.

- 1979b Studies in Macroeconomic Theory Vol. 1:
  Employment and Inflation.
  New York: Academic Press.

Phillips, A. W.
- 1958 "The Relation between Unemployment and the Rate of Change of Money Wage Rates in the United Kingdom, 1861-1957"
  Economica Vol. XXV, November, pp. 283-299.

Ritter, Lawrence S. and William L. Silber
1983 Principles of Money, Banking, and Financial Markets.
Fourth, Revised Edition.
New York: Basic Books.

1993 Principles of Money, Banking, and Financial Markets.
Eighth Edition.
New York: Basic Books.

Robinson, Joan
1973a "What has become of the Keynesian Revolution?"
in Robinson (1973b), Chapter 1, pp. 1-11.

1973b After Keynes. Edited by Joan Robinson.
Oxford: Basil Blackwell.

Rombach, Björn
1994 "Bilder fran en kommun i stormens öga"
("Pictures from a commune in the eye of the storm")
in Jacobsson, B. (Ed.) (1994).

Rothstein, Bo
1996 "Sa klarar vi jobben gratis"
("So can we solve the jobs gratis")
Dagens Nyheter October 13, DN Debatt, p. A4.

Rydén, Bengt and Villy Bergström (Eds.)
1982 Sweden, Choices for Economic and Social Policy
in the 1980s.
London: Allen & Unwin.

Samuelson, Paul A.
1973a "Monetarism Objectively Evaluated"
in Samuelson (1973b) pp. 120-129.
1973b Readings in Economics. Seventh edition.
New York: McGraw-Hill.

Scharpf, Fritz
   1991   Crisis and Choice in European Social Democracy.
           Ithaca, New York: Cornell University Press.

Scitovsky, Tibor
   1986   Human Desire and Economic Satisfaction:
           Essays on the Frontiers of Economics.
           Brighton, England: Wheatsheaf Books

   1992   The Joyless Economy:
           The Psychology of Human Satisfaction. Revised Edition.
           New York - Oxford: Oxford University Press.

   1995   Economic Theory and Reality:
           Selected Essays on their Disparities and Reconciliation.
           Aldershot, England: Edward Elgar

Sen, Amartya
   1970   Collective Choice and Social Welfare.
           San Francisco - Edinburgh: Holden-Day - Oliver & Boyd.

   1980   "Equality of What?" (The Tanner Lectures)
           in McMurrin (1980), pp. 195-219.

   1987a The Standard of Living:
           The Tanner Lectures, Clare Hall, Cambridge, 1985.
           With John Muellbauer, Ravi Kanbur, Keith Hart,
           Bernard Williams. Edited by Geoffrey Hawthorn.
           Cambridge: Cambridge University Press.

   1987b On Ethics and Economics.
           Oxford: Basil Blackwell.

   1993   "Capability and Well-Being"
           in Nussbaum and Sen (1993), pp. 30-53.

Shackle, G. L. S.
  1967 The Years of High Theory.
        Cambridge: Cambridge University Press.

Shepard, Stephen B.
  1997 "The New Economy: What It Really Means"
        Business Week November 17, pp. 48-50.

Sherman, Howard J. and Gary R. Evans
  1984 Macroeconomics. New York: Harper & Row.

Shonfield, Andrew
  1965 Modern Capitalism:
        The Changing Balance of Public and Private Power.
        Oxford: Oxford University Press.

  1984 In Defence of the Mixed Economy.
        Edited by Zuzanna Shonfield.
        Oxford: Oxford University Press.

Shultz, G. P. and R. Z. Aliber (Eds.)
  1966 Guidelines, Informal Controls, and the Market Place.
        Chicago: University of Chicago Press.

Small, D. and R. Porter
  1989 "Understanding the Behavior of M2 and V2"
        Federal Reserve Bulletin April.

Smelser, Neil J. and Richard Swedberg
  1994a "The Sociological Perspective on the Economy"
        in Smelser and Swedberg (1994b), Chapter 1, pp. 3-26.

  1994b Handbook of Economic Sociology
        Edited by Neil J. Smelser and Richard Swedberg.
        Princeton: Princeton University Press
        and Russell Sage Foundation.

Sollenius, Jan
  1983 Bridge-Building in Social Theory.
       Stockholm: Almqvist & Wiksell International.

  1992 The Middle of History?
       Stockholm: Almqvist & Wiksell International.

  1994 The End of Historical Projection:
       Essays in Social Theory.
       Stockholm: Almqvist & Wiksell International.

  1996 Decline of Deficits: Noninflationary Monetization.
       Stockholm: Almqvist & Wiksell International.

Solow, Robert M.
  1980 "On Theories of Unemployment"
       American Economic Review Vol. 70, No. 1 (March) pp. 1-11.

Soros, George
  1997 "Kapitalismen hotar demokratin"
       ("Capitalism threatens democracy")
       Dagens Nyheter January 15, Kultur pp. B 1-3.

Statistics Sweden
  1995 Statistisk Arsbok för Sverige '95
       (Statistical Yearbook of Sweden) Volume 81.
       Sveriges officiella statistik
       (Official Statistics of Sweden).
       Stockholm: Statistiska centralbyran.

  1998 Trender och prognoser '98
       ("Trends and prognoses '98").
       Stockholm: Statistiska centralbyran.

Statistics Sweden
　　1999　Statistisk Årsbok för Sverige '99
　　　　　(Statistical Yearbook of Sweden) Volume 85.
　　　　　Sveriges officiella statistik
　　　　　(Official Statistics of Sweden).
　　　　　Stockholm: Statistiska centralbyran.

Stephens, John D.
　　1996　"The Scandinavian Welfare States:
　　　　　Achievements, Crisis, and Prospects"
　　　　　in Esping-Andersen (1996d), Chapter 2, pp. 32-65.

Sternlight, Peter D.
　　1994　"The Implementation of Monetary Policy" in
　　　　　Colander and Daane (1994), Chapter 9, pp. 109-119.

Stiglitz, Joseph E. and Andrew Weiss
　　1981　"Credit Rationing in Markets with Imperfect Information"
　　　　　American Economic Review Vol. 71 (June) pp. 393-410.

Streeck, Wolfgang
　　1992　Social Institutions and Economic Performance:
　　　　　Studies of Industrial Relations
　　　　　in Advanced Capitalist Economies.
　　　　　London: Sage.

Sundelin, Inger
　　1999　"Låt inte e-posten styra dig"
　　　　　("Do not let the e-mail steer you")
　　　　　Dagens Nyheter February 25, p. IT 1.

Sveriges Riksbank
　　1995　"Monetary Policy Calendar"
　　　　　Quarterly Review No. 2, pp. 45-47.
　　　　　Stockholm: Sveriges Riksbank (The Swedish Central Bank).

Sveriges Riksbank
  1999   "Statistical Appendix"
         Quarterly Review No. 4, pp. 71-79.
         Stockholm: Sveriges Riksbank (The Swedish Central Bank).

Swedberg, Richard
  1990   Economics and Sociology: Redefining their boundaries:
         Conversations with Economists and Sociologists.
         Princeton: Princeton University Press.

  1991   "Major Traditions of Economic Sociology"
         Annual Review of Sociology Vol. 17, pp. 251-276.

  1993a "On the Relationship Between Economic Theory and Economic
         Sociology in the Work of Joseph Schumpeter"
         in Swedberg (1993b), Chapter 2, pp. 42-63.

  1993b Explorations in Economic Sociology
         Edited by Richard Swedberg.
         New York: Russell Sage Foundation.

  1996   Economic Sociology Edited by Richard Swedberg.
         Cheltenham, UK - Brookfield, US: Edward Elgar.

  1997   "New Economic Sociology:
         What Has Been Accomplished, What is Ahead?"
         Acta Sociologica Vol. 40, No. 2, pp. 161-182.

Swedberg, Richard and Mark Granovetter
  1992   "Introduction" in Granovetter and Swedberg (1992), pp. 1-26.

Tinbergen, J.
  1952   On the Theory of Economic Policy.
         Amsterdam: North-Holland.

Tobin, James
  1956   "The Interest Elasticity of Transactions Demand for Cash"
           Review of Economics and Statistics August.

  1970   "Money and Income: Post Hoc Ergo Propter Hoc?"
           Quarterly Journal of Economics May.

  1981   "The Monetarist Counter-Revolution Today - An Appraisal"
           Economic Journal Vol. 71, March.

  1987   Policies for Prosperity: Essays in a Keynesian Mode.
           Edited by P. M. Jackson.
           Brighton, England: Wheatsheaf Books.

Tomasson, Richard F.
  1970   Sweden: Prototype of Modern Society.
           New York: Random House.

U. S. Bureau of the Census
  1997   Statistical Abstract of the United States: 1997.
           117th edition. Washington, DC.

Vagerö, Denny
  1994   "Equity and Efficiency in Health Reform. A European View"
           Social Science & Medicine Vol. 39, No. 9, pp. 1203-1210.

  1995   "Health Inequalities As Policy Issues.
           Reflections on Ethic, Policy and Public Health"
           Sociology of Health & Illness Vol. 17, No. 1, pp. 1-19.

Venables, Tony
  1992   Amendment of the Treaties.
           Current EC Legal Development Series.
           London: Butterworths.

Weber, Max
   1978   Economy and Society Vol. I.
            Berkeley: University of California Press.

Weir, Margaret and Theda Skocpol
   1985   "State Structures and the Possibilities for
            'Keynesian' Responses to the Great Depression
            in Sweden, Britain, and the United States"
            in Evans, Rueschemeyer and Skocpol (Eds.) (1985),
            Chapter 4, pp. 107-163.

Wicksell, Knut
 (1898)   "The Influence of the Rate of Interest on Commodity Prices"
            English translation: in Wicksell (1958), pp. 67-89.

   1936   Interest and Prices:
            A Study of the Causes Regulating the Value of Money.
            (First published as Geldzins und Güterpreise,
            Jena: Gustav Fischer, 1898.)
            Translated by R. F. Kahn.
            With an Introduction by Prof. Bertil Ohlin.
            London: Macmillan.

   1958   Selected Papers on Economic Theory.
            Edited with an Introduction by Erik Lindahl.
            London: George Allen & Unwin.

Wolman, William and Anne Colamosca
   1997   The Judas Economy:
            The Triumph of Capital and the Betrayal of Work.
            Reading, Massachusetts - New York: Addison-Wesley.